HEALING
troubled
HEARTS
Daily Spiritual Exercises

LYN HOLLEY DOUCET

ST. ANTHONY MESSENGER PRESS
Cincinnati, Ohio

Excerpts from *Let Yourself Be Loved* by Phillip Bennett, copyright ©1997, Paulist Press, Inc., New York/Mahwah, N.J. Used with permission of Paulist Press.' www.paulistpress.com.

Brief quotation as submitted from *Addiction and Grace* by Gerald G. May, copyright ©1988 by Gerald G. May. Reprinted by permission of HarperCollins Publishers Inc.

Brief quotation as submitted from *The Wisdom of Tenderness* by Brennan Manning, copyright ©2002 by Brennan Manning. Reprinted by permission of HarperCollins Publishers Inc.

Brief quotation as submitted from *Care of the Soul* by Thomas Moore, copyright ©1992 by Thomas Moore. Reprinted by permission of HarperCollins Publishers Inc.

Excerpt from "We Cannot Measure How You Heal" by John Bell, copyright ©WGRG The Iona Community (Scotland). Used by permission of GIA Publications, Inc. All rights reserved. Printed in the U.S.A. 7404 S. Mason Ave., Chicago, IL 60638. www.giamusic.com. 800-442-1358.

Excerpt from "He Healed the Darkness of My Mind" by Fred Pratt Green is from *Gather*, Hope Publishing Company, p. 876.

Excerpt from *Letters to a Young Poet* by Rainer Maria Rilke, translated by M. D. Herter Norton. Copyright 1934, 1954 by W. W. Norton & Company, Inc., renewed ©1962, 1982 by M. D. Herter Norton. Used by permission of W. W. Norton & Company, Inc.

Cover and book design by Mark Sullivan

Library of Congress Cataloging-in-Publication Data

Doucet, Lyn Holley, 1950-
  Healing troubled hearts : daily spiritual exercises / Lyn Holley Doucet.
        p. cm.
  ISBN 0-86716-612-6 (alk. paper)
  1. Spiritual exercises. 2. Devotional calendars—Catholic Church. 3.
Catholic Church—Prayer-books and devotions—English. I. Title.
  BX2182.3.D68 2005
  248.8'6—dc22

                            2004027344

ISBN 0-86716-612-6

Copyright ©2005, by Lyn Holley Doucet. All rights reserved.

Published by St. Anthony Messenger Press
28 W. Liberty St.
Cincinnati, Ohio 45202
www.AmericanCatholic.org

Printed in U.S.A.
Printed on acid-free paper.

05 06 07 08 09 5 4 3 2 1

Acknowledgments

I believe in the power of Spirit who is moving through our world and bringing people and events together in wonderful ways. I experienced that Spirit when I rounded a corner at a National Pastoral Musician's convention and ran smack into Lisa Biedenbach, editorial director at St. Anthony Messenger Press. I had met Lisa before at other conferences but wasn't expecting to see her at this one. That meeting led to this book, as I was able to visit with her and other editors at St. Anthony Messenger Press during my stay in Cincinnati. They and I are so excited about the power of that same Spirit of Christ to heal troubled hearts in our world today.

Working with their professional staff, especially Kathleen Carroll, has been a joy and a privilege.

I want to acknowledge with all my heart those friends and directees who have allowed me to use their stories and especially Yvette, Barry, Chris, Ricky, Dale and Ginger— members of my original group experience.

As we share our stories with one another, we grow more human, more whole. We can be made part of the larger story that Christ came to tell: God loves us and wants us as his own.

Preface

Welcome to *Healing Troubled Hearts: Daily Spiritual Exercises*.

In our hyperactive world we long for peace and the knowing that comes from silence and prayer. We want to reach out to all that is so much larger than we are. And yet, we find it difficult to do so. There always seem to be other things that we need to do, places we need to go, money to earn, things to buy and obligations to meet.

It would be a shame, indeed, if all of our lives passed us by, and we didn't initiate an opportunity to go inward and learn both about ourselves and the God within and around us, who has loved us with an everlasting love. If we did take an inner journey, we might even dare to believe that God has a plan for our lives and has gifted us with exactly what we need to live out God's dream for us. In the silence of prayer we could hear the whispering magic of God's call.

Our wounds can keep us running from ourselves, from healing and from God's call. Negative voices within and without us drown out the simple sweet voice of Spirit. Perhaps this is the day you decide to stop for a while. Perhaps this is the day that you begin the most important retreat you will ever take. I will serve as innkeeper, but God is the retreat master. Go forward now in love, joy and peace.

Lyn Holley Doucet
Maurice, Louisiana

Notes on Journaling

I know of no better way to access your inner space than by journaling. This is free writing. Don't worry about grammar or spelling; just get your thoughts and feelings on paper. It is for you and God alone. The act of writing things down can free you from polluted inner space. Things become clearer. You get in touch with what you really believe and feel. Don't cheat yourself out of this opportunity.

Questions for reflection and journaling are included in each day's prayer materials. Try to do at least some of the journaling daily. There is no necessity to answer all the questions provided. Ample material is given so that you may choose the exercises that appeal to you. On some days you may complete only one question and that is just fine. This book exists for you and not you for this book!

Buy yourself a lovely journal, shop for a special pen, take up this book...and begin!

God has had a dream *of* me,
And *for* me, for all eternity.
It is a dream of healing and call,
Of life abundant with grace.
God fashioned me as an individual
To live an authentic life in community,
A life based on love.
Events in my life,
Within and without me,
Have warred against this authentic self of love.
My shadows have engulfed my gifts,
My Spirit-fire burns low, it smolders.
I can no longer find all the pieces of the person
God created me to be.
Perhaps it is all the happy fault,
This human path, this brokenness.
For now I seek Jesus the Healer, the Inspirer.
I want new eyes that open themselves to the reality
Of all that I was created to be.
Fully human, whole, not flawless,
Helping others and hoping with them.
I want to shine with God's light,
Especially through my broken places.
I desire to walk with freedom in God's Spirit.
I believe that God is still creating me today,
Resurrect me, my loving God.
Make me new again,
Able to give and to share,
In the abundant kingdom of the Risen One.

Table of Contents

OPTIONS FOR GROUP MEMBERS:

If you have longer than one week between group sessions, as most groups will, you can alternate this prayer format with other prayer forms, cover two-week portions of individual prayer, or allow multiple days for each day's lesson. There is a possibility that the group will decide to go more slowly through the material, even if they meet often. You will find here a number of prayer and meditation experiences as well as other activities. Remember that this is not about doing everything and doing it perfectly. It is about taking a journey, holding on to what you need and letting other things go, guided by the Sprit of God. I believe that the quality and quantity of prayer experiences and inner reflections in this book will give any individual or group options of richness and variety.

Introduction

O Jesus, my Beloved, who could express the tenderness
and sweetness with which You are guiding my soul! It
pleases you to cause the rays of Your grace to shine
through even in the mist of the darkest storm!
—Saint Thérèse of Lisieux

O Sing to the LORD a new song.
—Psalm 96:1

As I sit on my little porch in the early morning and look out
the large glass panes, I see the tomato plants that are now
past their prime and wilting. It is time to plant Louisiana
fall tomatoes, but who has the energy? Summer heat still
shimmers in the garden. Yet nature continues to renew herself. She waits serenely for what must die and what must
find new life.

A flock of white egrets flies high overhead in the slate
sky and their movement reminds me of fall, not quite come.
There is a subtle change in the air, a sweet feeling that the
near touch of autumn brings.

The first really cool day is a not too distant hope now;
perhaps summer will end after all. Although the calendar
marks January first as the beginning of the year, fall has
always spoken of new beginnings to me.

As a child I was always excited at this time of year, for
I loved the beginning of school. This time of year I had not
yet soiled my notebooks, lost my pencils, or left my book
sack in the classroom instead of taking it home. This would
be the year I would be organized! This would be the year I
would be neat! I would not daydream and miss directions! I

would *not* lose things. I would be like those immaculate girls I admired who seemed to have it all together.

The fact that I had this hope every year and the fact that I always lost all my pencils and messed up my notebooks by October never dissuaded my hopes. I still thrilled at the clean blank page and the new beginning. I always believed that this would be the year that things were different.

It was a good thing that despite disorganization and daydreaming, I was naturally good at the skills that schoolteachers valued, especially reading, and I could make good grades despite my many failings. Otherwise, I am sure I would not have welcomed the start of school so enthusiastically.

Perhaps you have similar (or mixed) feelings at the start of this journey, a journey into healing and conversion with yourself and others. Perhaps you vow that this will be the year that you will really pray, really give God and yourself the time you need. I hope you do have these feelings, for I believe that God works with our hopes and our intentions. Perhaps you are troubled because within your heart is a deep storm. Let yourself be wherever you are. For you will be relieved to know that this is a journey about wholeness, not about perfection. Certainly we will not always pray as we would like. We will struggle and have dryness in prayer; we may even want to give up. If our pains are deep, it may be difficult to imagine ourselves praying at all. We may feel we should "get our act together" before we come to God. But all that is needed is that we come as we are, and we embrace ourselves as we are. In fact, honesty with self and others is a key to this journey.

We need to share our perceived faults as well as our perceived successes and virtues, for much of our selves are hidden from our own view and many of our perceptions are flawed. Jesus advised against the rooting out of faults. He knew that sometimes we could not tell the difference between our failings and our strengths. He advised us to turn to the Master Gardener in prayer and to seek more understanding before judging ourselves too harshly.

I ask that God, Mother Mary and all the angels support you in this journey of discovery. Be gentle with yourself and give to yourself the love you learn to offer to others.

For my experience has shown me that when we lose all our pencils or mess up our notebooks (or our relationships), God loves us all the more. He reaches out to us in tenderness and says, "Let me help you. I long to bring the good in your life to fruition. Place yourself in my hands."

Part One: Individual Prayer

Week One

LOOKING AHEAD: BEGINNING A PRAYER JOURNEY

During this first week, we seek a time and place to pray.
We embrace surrender, awareness and trust.
Seeing ourselves as chosen for this journey.
We open ourselves to God's touch of love.
God seeks us; we are precious.
We have run away.
We ask for God's mercy.

Week One: Day One

SPACIOUSNESS: FINDING A TIME AND A PLACE TO PRAY

> I must have time, space and quiet for this gestation to occur.
> —Joyce Rupp, *The Star in my Heart*

> But I, through the abundance of your steadfast love,
>> Will enter your house
> —Psalm 5:7

I love to walk into a neat, clean and ordered room. When I do, I feel my spirit expand so that peace and silence can fill me. When I tidy a room, a new spaciousness opens up, as do new possibilities. With clutter removed I see things in a new, optimistic light.

Spaciousness in our lives is what we need to nurture new life as we work with this book. This spaciousness connotes a gentle and flowing order, without rigidity. We need to open up our time, our living space and our hearts in a new way for our healing journey.

Many of us know the importance of having a space of our own to enter and to pray, to just *be*. During this special time, we need to reclaim that special space, a home for our souls, where we can go and be quiet. This is a place where we can listen. Perhaps we need only a bedroom corner and a comfortable chair. There may be a table where we have placed a candle and an icon or statue. A rarely used formal dining room fills the need for others. Other family members should know that this is our space for prayer. When we enter and light a candle, we have entered holy ground, and we are enclosed with God, fully open to Spirit.

When do we find time alone? Is it early in the morning, when we rise in darkness and open our heart to the Spirit?

Spiritual writer Gary Zukav calls this "Earth time." We are still tied to the earth by sleep, and the raucous world has not yet entered our consciousness. This is the time of deep waking dreams and a lovely spirit connection. I know that I feel gentleness and an inner quiet when I pray early in the morning.

Do we choose to pray in an empty chapel at lunchtime? An unused room in the office building? A quiet place in a park for prayer and journaling? An apple and some cheese satisfy our hunger when we are filled with God.

We may wait until evening when all is quiet, turning our thoughts to God and to birthing this new life within us. Whatever the time or place, we are committed to the process, and we try again when we fail.

As I write these words, a soft rain falls upon a boundless earth. The gentle earth teaches us that there is a time and a place for everything. Deep in the soil are all the dormant seeds, waiting for the warmth of spring, and there is space for everyone. The earth makes room for all her creations: rabbit and birds, grasses and clovers, trees and black-nosed raccoons.

God fashioned a creation of uniqueness and beauty, and we are an important, vital part of God's creation. Just as within the acorn is all the potential of the mighty oak, so within us is the potential of a unique and beautiful nature, a special spirit given to us alone. In the great heart of God is everything necessary for our growth. We need but claim it; open ourselves to the blessings God longs to bestow. Let us begin today in a new way.

FOR REFLECTION AND JOURNALING

+ Where can you have a secure and quiet place to pray?
+ When is the best time of day for your prayer?

+ What are your feelings as you begin this journey of prayer?

CLOSING PRAYER

Let God speak to your heart…O my beloved, abide under the shelter of the lattice for I have betrothed you to Myself, and though you are sometimes indifferent toward me, my love for you is at all times as a flame of fire. My ardor never cools. My longing for your love and affection is deep and constant.

—Frances J. Roberts, *Come Away My Beloved*

Week One: Day Two

GOD IS SEEKING AFTER US

> Which one of you, having a hundred sheep and losing one of them, does not leave the ninety-nine in the wilderness and go after the one that is lost until he finds it? When he has found it, he lays it on his shoulders and rejoices. And when he comes home, he calls together his friends and neighbors, saying to them, "Rejoice with me, for I have found my sheep that was lost."
> —Luke 15:4–6

We have begun our healing journey by seeking a place and a time to pray. Perhaps we are realizing this at this moment: we are in our special place and the time has come for us to open our hearts to God's care. Now we look at our attitudes toward God and God's work within us. I want to assure you that work with these daily spiritual exercises is not really all about work at all! Allow me to make a comparison.

I have a guilty secret, which is that I think I weigh a good bit more than I look like I do! I guess I still look thin, because people are always telling me that I look like I have lost weight or ask me how I stay so trim. These comments come despite the fact that my scale has been moving steadily up for several years. Therefore, after Christmas when the scales tipped up even further, and my jeans (I already went up a size) got very hard to zip, I said, "This is it. I must cut back on my eating!" If this sounds like vanity, it is. Vanity dances around in my shadow and often invades my persona. It is the vanity of insecurity, not pride.

So like folks all over the country, I hit the gym more and pushed away the butter and mayonnaise. I even gave away the Christmas fudge! This weight loss thing is a self-improvement project, and I have taken charge!

Healing the soul is nothing like this, nothing at all. Instead of taking charge, we relinquish it. We open ourselves in surrender, a very counter-cultural thing to do.

In the parable of the lost sheep, the sheep is doing nothing at all but being lost. All the initiative is left to the Shepherd who is ardently seeking his sheep. Of course, the sheep could have remained hidden and run from the shepherd's voice. It could have stayed in the wilderness and refused to come home. But sheep are smarter than that.

As we begin our journey, know that the one we seek is already ardently seeking us. God longs to help and to heal. Harold S. Kushner tells us, "We may be so busy taking care of things that we neglect our souls."[1] This is when we wander far away from the one who loves us. This is when God walks through the wilderness of our hearts to bring us home.

FOR REFLECTION AND JOURNALING

+ Read the passage about the lost sheep (Luke 15:4–6) in your Bible. Write down those words that speak to your heart.
+ In what ways do you feel lost?

+ Are you in touch with your hurting or "desert" feelings?
+ What within you resists surrender to God's care?

CLOSING PRAYER

Great Heart within me and about me,
Help me to believe that I am so uniquely precious to you,
That you would go wandering in the desert looking for me,
Leaving the ninety-nine.
I guess my small heart can't quite wrap around it,
I can't understand my value to you.
Help me to surrender all those things I thought I knew
about myself,
Into my Shepherd's gentle care.

Week One: Day Three

CHOSEN FOR GOD'S KINGDOM OF LOVE

> You did not choose me but I chose you.
> —John 15:16

> It's my God, too, my Bible, my church, my faith; it chose
> me. But it does not make me "chosen" in a way that
> would exclude others. I hope it makes me eager to
> recognize the good, and the holy, whenever I encounter it.
> —Kathleen Norris, *Amazing Grace*

Yesterday we looked at developing an attitude of surrender, or releasing ourselves into God's care, the way a sheep would turn toward his shepherd. We can only begin to surrender when we feel safe, when we develop trust in God to care for our needs.

When our lives are chaotic and things are not working as we would wish, this trust is harder to develop. Developing this trust will be a part of working with this book and looking deeply at your life, your choices. The paradox for us as Christians is that in the midst of a broken world, we find, as Father Richard Rohr says, that the universe is friendly and that no matter the external conditions —we are safe.

So even now, early in this process, I ask you to take this a step further and to embrace not only surrender and trust but an attitude of being *chosen*. Depending on where you are in your life, you might want to say, "What? Chosen for this? Could I be unchosen, please?"

This morning I smile as I remember my friend Teenie who was attending a Catholic school in the sixties. Teenie very much wanted to marry and have children, and so she wondered about the sisters who taught her. *Why had they become religious sisters?* She asked one of the nuns this question and the dear lady said, "My child, I was chosen by God." Shaken to her core, Teenie then ran into the hall and leaned against the wall praying with all her might, "God, don't choose me! Don't choose me!"

Ah, but God puts the desires in our heart for what is to be our path in life. (Teenie did indeed marry and have children.) Part of this process you now begin is to get in touch with those very desires.

If your life is going smoothly at present, the knowledge of being chosen may feel, well, just *right* to you. I have often shied away from this word, because I don't like the idea of my being chosen by God if someone else is left out. But it doesn't mean this at all. It only means that we allow ourselves to be open to God's voice, God's unique call in our lives.

I had an intuitive experience of feeling chosen one afternoon, as I struggled to bring order to this book you are reading. A long session of cross-outs and unsatisfactory rewrites had left me wondering about my vocation as writer. Then later I was able to make this journal entry...

> *As I sit on the porch this afternoon, waking from a nap, the sun breaks through the clouds and casts a soft almond light over everything, in a last burst before setting. I suddenly feel blessed, somehow chosen to be at this very place and see this very light. Chosen to wrestle with these specific words and write this unique book.*
>
> *It occurs to me then, that this promise of being chosen is real. Jesus clearly states in John 15 that he has chosen us to be grafted to the vine that is himself. That this vine is to bring us love and health, and flower us into the very kingdom of God that we seek.*

I ask you to consider that the fact that you are doing this inner work indicates your beginning embrace of being chosen. As you pray and spend time seeking God, you become more firmly grafted onto the vine that is Christ and more open to the Spirit within you.

FOR REFLECTION AND JOURNALING

+ In the chaotic and calm events of your life, do you recognize that you have been chosen?
+ How do you recognize the good and holy when you see it?
+ How does it help you become what you seek to become?
+ How do you claim God's goodness for yourself? What are you claiming today?

CLOSING PRAYER

God, make me a healthy branch
Of your ever-flourishing vine.
I want the greenness of your love,
Flowing into me. Refreshing me,

Allowing me to see beauty and goodness everywhere.
May I dare to believe that you have chosen me?
And that if I surrender my life to you,
That all will be well.
Amen.

Week One: Day Four

AWARENESS AND OPENNESS

> Then Jesus said to him, "What do you want me to do
> for you?" The blind man said to him, "My teacher, let
> me see again."
> —Mark 10:51

> O Divine Presence,
> I do not enter the deeper realm
> All by myself.
> Always you are there with me,
> As a Guide to protect and direct me,
> As a Loving Companion to embrace and support me,
> As a Wise one to provide both challenge and solace.
> —Joyce Rupp, *Dear Heart, Come Home*

> I am a feather on the breath of God.
> —Hildegard of Bingen

In previous days we have looked at our attitudes toward the spiritual journey: the trust needed to surrender, and the knowledge of ourselves as chosen in God's sight. As we begin to pray daily, we ask for a new awareness to come into our lives—a new seeing. We seek to see more deeply into things, and to know that the surface of things is not all there is. We pray to know how God is working in our lives, how God is reaching out through people and events and nature to heal us and bring us home.

For the past year or so, I have been taking walks in the sugarcane field behind my house. This is a special place for me now and when I hop over the ditch and enter the turn row, I feel that I am in a different world. The sugarcane field reflects all the changes in nature as the seasons progress: the tiny green shoots in spring, the billowing of hearty green in summer, the harvest of fall. A few days ago I walked there into a wonderful flurry of yellow butterflies that filled the rows and dipped into the rainwater held by little hollows in the earth. I was aware that nature—God's world—is intensely beautiful and filled to bursting with good things. This knowledge gives me courage as I look at visions of war and suffering on my television screen. I allow myself to live in paradox and to embrace my questions about the way God works in our world. If I allow it, the delicate, floating butterflies and the cane field that embraces them open me to the wonder of God's providence.

Author Paula D'Arcy says it this way: "So much is hidden from me. Hidden right in front of my nose, and directly in my line of sight. But I will not see it until I am able to look from a different place and am ready to know what I have not yet considered."[2]

Jesus healed hurting people so many years ago, and I believe that he still longs to heal our wounds and blindness if we but ask. Our faults are hidden from us, it is true, but so is the goodness within us. We believe we are what others have told us we are. We think that the world is the way others have *told* us it is. We don't know that there is so much more.

FOR REFLECTION AND JOURNALING

Don't worry about working on becoming more aware. This kind of new seeing comes slowly and gently. We don't have to figure it out. Jesus still heals our inner eyes, the eyes of the blind. All we need to do is surrender and ask for the gift of a new awareness: to see God shining in everything and everyone, especially now within ourselves. As our journey continues, we will receive the light in new ways and recognize the Companion who brings us home.

+ What are you feeling as you begin this process?

+ What do you hope to see within yourself?

+ Do you feel resistance to being hopeful about your own healing and restoration? Explain.

+ Do you think you are as open to and aware of the beauty and goodness about you as you? Is it easier for you to notice things and circumstances that you perceive as negative or painful? Explain.

CLOSING PRAYER

Hildegard of Bingen, Lord,
said that she was a feather on the breath of God.
Like the yellow butterfly she rose and fell gracefully with the currents of life.
What within me resists this graceful dance?
How am I closed? Where do I lack awareness?
Help me to see again, to really see the ways that I myself make life difficult.
Now I dare to believe that you are speaking to me, Lord.
Give me the openness to hear you!
Give me the trust that accepts and embraces all that is.
Amen.

Week One: Day Five

SILENCE

> I will come to you in the silence,
> I will lift you from all your fear.
> —David Haas, *You Are Mine*

> Allow yourself simply to be, in stillness of heart and
> mind, before God, whose face is shining upon you,
> warming you into eternal life. Be present to him, as he
> is to you, simply absorbing his love and his grace.
> —Margaret Silf, *Inner Compass*

> The things that help us get back to integrated knowing
> are obvious, and are not obvious at all. Silence is
> helpful, especially extended silence where we observe
> ourselves and can feel the changes taking place. We
> can feel emotional changes, moment by moment. In
> quiet times we can tell what anger feels like in our
> body. Maybe that's why we avoid quiet times.
> —Richard Rohr, *Everything Belongs*

We have now offered ourselves the spaciousness of time and
a place to pray, and opened ourselves to God's love and healing. I would like us now to consider another important com-
ponent of our healing prayer journey: the cultivation of
silence. Every spiritual tradition speaks of the sacredness
of silence, a silence of our prayer environment outside of us
and of our spirits within us.

Having an empty nest makes it much easier for me to
live in more silence. I don't have my son coming and going
with his music and his friends in tow asking what there is
to eat. I certainly enjoyed those days, but they are gone. I
rarely turn on the television during the day, and I live in the

country with enough seclusion that the noises of the world are muted. I am fortunate, and I have come to prefer the quiet in a deep sort of way, like preferring a thick, home-made vegetable soup to a fast-food hamburger. Silence is delicious, sustaining and health-giving.

I even feel a little disconcerted now when I go into a noisy house with one or two televisions going, Game Boys popping and telephones ringing constantly. I confess to wanting to control another's space! I want to reach out and turn things off! However, I understand that this is the reality that many, maybe most, families in our country live with. We have grown accustomed to higher levels of noise, and lots and lots of activity. This impacts us all. Quite recently I tried to enjoy the movie *Thérèse* while a lady in front of me chatted a bit on her cell phone!

Yet the truth is that all this noise and activity drowns out God's silent and still voice, the voice that drifts in on the gentlest of breezes. We no longer hear the cries of our own souls.

During this first week you might want to consider the noisiness of your life. You may want to turn off the radio in your car or turn the television on later in the day. Try sitting outside and letting the healing sounds of nature fill you. If you begin to practice silence, you will reap peace as your reward. You are on a special healing journey. Take some blessed silence along with you.

FOR REFLECTION AND JOURNALING
+ What brings a lot of noise into your life?
+ How could you have more silence there?
+ Have you ever experienced the blessings of silence, perhaps on a retreat? Write about what you felt then.
+ Can you spend five minutes sitting quietly and doing nothing but breathing gently? Give this a try. Over the

next days and weeks, try to increase the time you can sit quietly like this.

CLOSING PRAYER

God, you come to me in the silence,
And I stop to listen, stop to hear you.
Quiet down the chatter of my heart and mind.
Help me listen all through the day.
May my spirit become a cool and clear pool
of still and silent water.
May I reflect the goodness of your loving face
in my deepest parts.
Amen.

Week One: Day Six

LEARNING TO REST IN PRAYER

> Therefore the Lord waits to be gracious to you;
>> Therefore he will rise up to show mercy to you.
> —Isaiah 30:18

> Is not my heart drawn out toward you to bless you?
> —Frances J. Roberts, *Come Away My Beloved*

The attitudes and the circumstances that we seek for our prayer lives can be expressed today in the experience of centering prayer. Today we will reverently approach this prayer of quiet. Don't skip over this part of the week; it is vital to the process. Read over all the instructions first and then relax and put them into use. If you have never done this type of prayer, it may be a little disconcerting at first. Don't be afraid. God will reward any effort on your part. Can you just sit with God and let him love you for some minutes?

INSTRUCTIONS FOR PRAYER

(Spend ten to fifteen minutes doing this.)

Light a candle and relax.

Let your mind and heart grow still.

Ask God to bless your journey.

Then just spend some time in his loving presence.

Just breathe in and out and be with God.

Breathe out all tension and stress,

Breathe in love and peace.

Let the thoughts of your mind flow by,

Don't try to stop them or hold on to them.

Just let everything be.

If inner resistance arises (I must get up and do something)

Just love it and be with in, don't give in to it.

God is with you, loving you, now.

There is nothing more important that you could be doing.

Than receiving this love.

Ask the Divine Physician to heal your hurting places,

And quiet your troubled mind.

Experience the Love that changes everything.

FOR REFLECTION AND JOURNALING

+ What was your experience today with this type of prayer?
  What thoughts and feelings did you have on this day?
+ How can you bring this quiet into the rest of your day?
+ Would this be a prayer form you would like to practice?
  Explain.

CLOSING PRAYER

Gracious Healer, God of light,

I come to you today, humbly aware of my need for healing
and conversion of heart.

I have been blind in many ways, and hurting.

Sometimes my blindness and pain hurts others.

But sometimes, I have been the victim
Of another's blindness.
Life has left its mark upon me. I bear its scars.
I want to change and heal, and be closer to you.
I desire that whatever is holding me fast be loosened.
That light will shine brightly
Upon any darkness I have in my heart.
That this sweet light will set me free.
Amen.

Week One: Day Seven

ABUNDANT LIFE: SEEING BENEATH THE SURFACE

> On this narrow planet, we have only the choice
> between two unknown worlds. One of them tempts us—
> ah! what a dream to live in that!—the other stifles us.
> —Sidonie-Gabrielle Colette

> I came that they may have life, and may have it more
> abundantly
> —John 10:10

A recent inquiry posed in a Bible study was, "Name a time that you have unjustly judged someone by her appearance." One of the women in the group said wryly and truthfully, "All the time, all the time."

I remember when my little niece saw the movie *Shrek* and said cheerfully, "So the point is that the way you look doesn't matter." I didn't disillusion her, but our society does little to express this truth. It is so easy for *our* lives to become centered on what we have, how we look, our images and the face we show to the world. The cry of our cultural consciousness is not only, "Give us more!" it is, "Give us more that looks better!" I sometimes enjoy the new "makeover" shows on television, but I get uneasy when we redesign our physical bodies through great expense and pain as if they were all that mattered to our happiness and authenticity.

That's why I congratulate you on this *inner* journey. Believe me, it's countercultural! In your own way, you're a revolutionary! Taking a deep, slow and long journey within is done by few. And yet, it is there that Jesus stands, offering abundant life for those who seek him with all their hearts. We can choose this life today, a different way of being.

Look over your journaling for the week. In what ways is your spirit stifled and compressed? In what ways does life in Christ beckon you? You may want to highlight some of the themes that are emerging for you. How is your prayer progressing?

Closing Prayer
Holy Spirit,
I embrace spaciousness: make it more and more present in my life.
I seek silence: let it become as natural to me as breathing.
I open myself in trust: meet me with your strong, supporting love.
I open my eyes in awareness: fill them with your light.
I allow myself to be chosen by your grace: heal the unworthiness within me.
Guide me during the week to come. I love you. Amen.

Week Two

Looking Within: A Spiritual Checkup

Now that we have found a time, a place and an openness to
prayer,
We consider the landscape of our inner lives.
We seek the places where quiet waters sparkle,
And places where the darkness wants to yield
all the things that darkness knows.
We traverse this landscape knowing
That we are not alone.

Week Two: Day One

A SPIRITUAL CHECKUP

> ...be patient toward all that is unsolved in your heart
> and try to love the *questions themselves* like locked
> rooms and like books that are written in a very foreign
> tongue. Do not now seek the answers, which cannot be
> given you because you would not be able to live
> them....*Live* the questions now. Perhaps you will then
> gradually, without noticing it, live along some distant
> day into the answer.
> —Rainer Maria Rilke, *Letters to a Young Poet*

Some months ago I devised this spiritual checkup as part of a retreat. It has been one of the most requested handouts that I have ever written. Perhaps it gives a way to begin to understand our own hearts.

Take some time some over the next four days to complete this spiritual checkup. It will give you some knowledge of where you might want to go on this journey of discovery.

SPIRITUAL CHECKUP

We sometimes go to the doctor for a physical checkup. Often we know something is not quite right, or we may just need assurance that we are well. We may need to make adjustments in lifestyle and behavior, or seek help from others.

In the same way, periodically, we should give ourselves a spiritual checkup. For it is rare that we take the time to examine our lives under this light.

A note of caution: This process is not about beating yourself up. We know we are good at being critical of ourselves. It is about love and hope: God loves us unconditionally.

FOR REFLECTION AND JOURNALING

+ Do you have a prayer time set aside daily or several times a week? Has this practice changed recently with the use of this book? Explain.

+ In general, how do you pray (set prayers, Scripture, rosary)? Are you responding to other forms of prayer now? In what ways?

+ At present, are you in a period of dryness, or warmth and closeness in prayer? Explain.

+ How do you nourish the creative spirit within you? How would you like to?

CLOSING PRAYER

Precious Spirit,
Headaches and heartaches sometimes haunt my days.
At other times I can be with you in peace and calm and love.
Show me the pathways through all of my life: the darkness and the light,
The sadness and pain,
The lightness of joy.
Be my Physician, my Companion and my Guide.
Never leave my side, I pray.
Amen.

Week Two: Day Two

FINDING OUR STYLE: CONTINUING THE SPIRITUAL CHECKUP

> None of us will keep up a life of prayer unless we are prepared to change. We will either give it up, or turn it into a little system that maintains the form of godliness but denies the power of it—which is the same thing as giving it up.
>
> —Richard J. Foster, *Prayer: Finding the Heart's True Home*

I can get overwhelmed when I spend days in large groups. My mind begins to race too much, and I feel nervous and uncentered. One factor is that I easily absorb the emotions of any group. My spiritual director has been working with me on meditations to prevent this, but sometimes I forget to use them!

Although I test out as an extravert on psychological tests, I am just barely one. I have many qualities of the introvert. For me, spending down-time is a must. Regrouping within through quiet prayer, walking alone, or even reading an uplifting and well-written novel centers and refocuses me. So as you continue your spiritual checkup today, if you are lacking peace in your life, you may want to consider the reasons why. Think about your personality and your innate gifts. Are you living a life attuned to them?

We begin today, also, to consider our deeply held images of God. It is difficult for us to trust a God who we may perceive as judging, distant and cold. Sometimes we cling to images of God that we formed as children. Then God loses real power in our lives.

Some the reasons for our distance from God may be exterior, others interior. If you don't have time to do all of these reflections in your journal today, hold the questions in your heart. The answers will unfold as you live your days.

FOR REFLECTION AND JOURNALING
+ What is your usual image of God? Write about this.
+ Who taught you the most about God? Reflect upon what was taught to you. Do you still agree with these teachings?
+ Do you often do things you enjoy? Why or why not?
+ In general, do you feel at peace? Do you know why or why not? Explain.
+ Do you often get irritated and/or feel rushed and harried? Why or why not?

CLOSING PRAYER

Lord, I thank you for the opportunity
To visit my heart and soul today.
To learn more about my self: my habits, my feelings, my prayer.
I want to learn more about my attitudes toward you.
I want a bigger God than I have crafted before.
Let me believe that you love me as I am, that I do not have to change for you to love me.
I thank you. I love you. Amen.

Week Two: Day Three

LIVING ON THE ROAD: THE SPIRITUAL CHECKUP CONTINUES

> "The classroom is on the road," Jesus says, "You'll learn to love by touching the unloved. You'll learn to handle hurt by walking into hurt. You'll learn to be a disciple by walking with me, even when you feel afraid and ill prepared. You'll learn to bear fruit by bearing fruit. Rise. Follow me."
>
> —John Coleman, *The Unexpected Teachings of Jesus*

I recently went to drop off some groceries at our local women's and children's shelter. Security there is very tight, and I usually don't see any of the guests. As I headed back to my car, in the window above me there appeared a tiny child of about three or so. He was a little boy with dark hair and eyes, dressed in yellow shorts and a white T-shirt. He looked down at me and slowly waved his little hand. As I got into my car, my eyes filled with tears as I pondered the violence and pain this little fellow had already experienced. I prayed that he and his mother would find enough support to fashion a better life.

Think about your own community of friends and worshippers today. Think about the forms of service in your life as well.

FOR REFLECTION AND JOURNALING

+ What is your worship or spiritual community? Are you still searching? Have you suffered brokenness and loss around this issue? What gifts do you receive in community?
+ In what forms of service do you reflect your faith?
+ Do you find it easy or difficult to work in service with others? Explain.

CLOSING PRAYER

Lord,
I remember that
Saint Paul said, "Let all things be done in a way that will build up the community."
Let me be a community builder, O God.
No matter how small my community,
no matter how humble my task,
may I do it with love.
Amen.

Week Two: Day Four

RECOGNIZING WOUNDEDNESS: COMPLETING THE SPIRITUAL CHECKUP

Blessed are the poor in spirit, for theirs is the kingdom of heaven.
—Matthew 5:3

Shout to us ever more loudly, God of All Blessedness, about those you call blessed. Let us not forget your love

for the poor, the mourning, the hungry, the
peacemakers. As we acknowledge and speak honestly of
our hurt feelings, heal us.
—Gaynell Cronin and Jack Rathschmidt, O.F.M. Cap.,
The Blessing Candles

Light a candle in your sacred prayer space and invite the
spirit of God to be with you.

As we complete the spiritual checkup today, we ask that
God gently begin to show us where our woundedness is
holding us back from receiving our full measure of God's
peace, joy and energy. Take this slowly. You may want to
acknowledge only that there are wounds. It may not be the
time to explore them in any way. This scarring may show up
in our relationships. We may have depression or anxiety, or
even numerous physical problems. Hold your wounds with
love today. Oh, my friends, I pray so deeply that you love
yourself as God loves you as you continue this process.

FOR REFLECTION AND JOURNALING

+ Most of us encounter differing relationship "climates."
  Describe in general terms the relationships in your life
  that are the most rewarding, the most peaceful, the most
  stressful. Do you have, or have you been impacted by relationships that were toxic and harmful?
+ Are you aware of wounds within you that hinder your
  relationships with God, yourself and others? Explain
  briefly if desired.
+ Are you growing in self-acceptance? If yes, what has
  helped you? If no, in what ways have you been hindered?
+ Do you feel that you have a loving, personal relationship
  with Jesus? Why or why not?
+ As you proceed in your work with this book, what do you
  hope to gain from these spiritual exercises?

CLOSING PRAYER

Lord, as I grow in the landscape of relationships.

Graft me onto your vine,

Fertilize me with your life.

Grow me larger, warmer; let my roots go deeper into your good earth.

So that I am healthier, stronger in wholeness, filled with peace.

Please show me the way to the healing and love that I seek.

Amen.

Week Two: Day Five
HOPE

> When one puts all his care on God, and rests wholly upon Him, being careful, meanwhile to serve him faithfully, God takes cares of him; and the greater the confidence of such a one, the more the care God extends over him; neither is there any danger of its failing, for God has an infinite love for those souls that repose in him.
> —Saint Francis De Sales

> I am new inside today. I feel pink and tender as if young tissue were growing within. I have been willing to take an ultimate risk by looking at the state of my life and insides, not as I wish they were but as they actually are.
> —Tian Dayton, *Daily Affirmations for Forgiving and Moving On*

Congratulations on completing your spiritual checkup. Perhaps you are very happy with what has been revealed. Perhaps like many of us, dismay is the emotion you feel. Making time and space to truly live and breathe our faith is not always easy. But we should never live in discouragement, because this is not something that we trudge about doing in aloneness. All that is asked of us is an increasing openness and willingness to place ourselves at God's disposal—a growing trust. When we begin to do this, even in the wildest storms of life hope springs up within us.

In southern Louisiana we are famous for our food, our music, our culture and our hurricanes. During Hurricane Lilly, a friend of mine uncovered hope in a profound and new way. The morning after the hurricane roared through, Monique was in her backyard, and her feelings were as gray as the overhead clouds as she surveyed the scene. Most of the large, mature shade trees in her yard had been uprooted. Her carefully tended beds of flowers and evergreens were destroyed. She thought ruefully of all the picnics and outdoor events that she and her family had enjoyed in this backyard. Memories stretched back over the years.

Even the children's tree house had been dashed to the ground. She tried to be thankful that her house had sustained only minor damage, but she didn't feel thankful. She felt uprooted herself from much she had known and cherished.

Then, turning, she caught her breath as she saw her Cherokee rosebush. It was completely intact and filled numerous plump buds, and, wonder of wonders, sported one flawless and fully opened flower. How had it survived? And just as she pondered this, the sun came out and just for a moment rested upon the yellow petals scattered beneath the bush. They reflected the sunlight like gold. Monique's heart suddenly filled with hope. She felt as though the light on the rosebush was bringing her a message: do not despair; all will be well.

Our spiritual checkup may have shown us that we are lacking in hope. We need to take hope firmly by the hand as we journey together in prayer. Today, offer these gifts to the God of hope: your fatigue, your sadness, your dissatisfaction, your fear. Ask God to hold and warm them for you. When you are ready, you can look closely at all these things; for now, just center yourself in hope. God is with you.

Like Monique, we will live in the whirlwind, but, as Raissa Maritain says, while we risk bruising ourselves against a thousand obstacles, we also trust in God as our light. To be closer to God and others is the reason we check on our inner lives.

FOR REFLECTION AND JOURNALING

+ Journal about the feelings and questions that your spiritual checkup has uncovered.
+ What steps can you take to begin to answer your questions?
+ Where are the "hurricanes" in your life?
+ Where is the hope in your life?

CLOSING PRAYER

My Savior,
All these questions. What can they mean? Will I sort through them?
Will I learn to live with them?
Be with me now, in hurricane places,
and sweet, peaceful spaces.
Be with me now and bring your golden gift
of hope. Amen.

Week Two: Day Six

RESTING AND BEING IN OUR GOD

Christ manifests himself differently in each of us. Each of us has a unique role in the life of the universe, to let

> God be God in our particular circumstances, in our
> time, in our circle of people. No one can take our place.
> No higher destiny is possible.
> —Gerard W. Hughes, *Seven Weeks for the Soul*

We have already spent many days of prayer examining our habits, our exterior lives, and beginning to look at our woundedness. Today as all of our prayer percolates within us, let us rest in God. He will do the work within us. Today we praise him. We invite him fully in to be with us, all during our day.

Read the words of this psalm slowly, stopping when certain phrases speak to your heart. Write these special words in your journal as they speak to you. Read the psalm again and reflect deeply upon it. What might God be telling you? Live with these words today.

> For God alone my soul waits in silence;
>> for my hope is from him.
> He alone is my rock and my salvation,
>> my fortress; I shall not be shaken.
> On God rests my deliverance and my honor;
>> my mighty rock, my refuge is in God.
> Trust in him at all times, O people;
>> pour out your heart before him;
>> God is a refuge for us.
> —Psalm 62:5–8

FOR REFLECTION AND JOURNALING

+ What words of the psalm spoke to you? Explain.
+ In what or whom do you place your trust?
+ What areas of my life need to be turned over to God's care?
+ To what degree do you rely on God in making everyday decisions?

CLOSING PRAYER
Embracing God, your knowledge will trace
The light within me and the hidden place,
Where fear and boredom lodge.
Enliven me, I pray. Give me rivers of hope,
that slake the thirst within.
Give me your courage and your life.
I know there is more meaning to my journey
than just what I see.
Let us sit together and drink deeply.
Tell me about trusting you,
tell me about your love.
Amen.

Week Two: Day Seven

SPIRITUAL GUMBO

> Because the purpose of our lives is built into every cell
> of our bodies, we don't need to look far to find it. We
> can find it by looking near, in the little everyday things
> that give us consolation or desolation. I experience
> consolation when I see the leaves of a plant turn
> toward the sun, when I sense the vitality in whole
> foods as I prepare them, when I feel the life energy in
> natural cotton clothing…to recognize the face of God in
> all things.
> —Sheila Fabricant-Linn, *Sleeping with Bread*

> Then he [Elisha] lay down under the broom tree and fell
> asleep. Suddenly an angel touched him and said to him,
> "Get up and eat." He looked, and there at his head was
> a caked baked on hot stones, and a jar of water. He ate
> and drank, and lay down again. The angel of the LORD

came a second time, touched him, and said, "Get up and eat, otherwise the journey will be too much for you."
—1 Kings 19:5–7

Our journey is unfolding. We have had the courage to begin to look deeply within and, hopefully, the courage to trust God with our spiritual healing. Perhaps the purpose of our lives is calling to us. Perhaps hope and discouragement dance within us, side by side. Perhaps we are partaking of "Spiritual Gumbo."

The weather was drizzling and cold yesterday when I arrived home, chilled and weary, to find a savory pot of gumbo simmering on the stove. This unexpected treat was provided by my Cajun cook husband, Dee. Its warmth filled me.

When I was growing up, my parents made what I now call Baton Rouge gumbo, but others call Creole gumbo. It contained stewed tomatoes and slices of okra, and I loved it. My husband makes a simple, earthy Cajun gumbo that features dark roux (for those not from Louisiana, this is flour and oil mixed and cooked to a rich, shiny darkness and plied with chopped onions and other seasonings), rich broth, seasonings and lots of sliced green onions and fresh parsley. Served over fluffy steamed rice it is hard to beat. (Pass the hot sauce!)

There are many ways to make gumbo, and most are delicious. However, I don't order gumbo in a restaurant unless someone recommends it, or I know for sure what I am getting. Some cooks take interpretation too far!

This journey is like gumbo: There isn't just one recipe. There are not certain things one must feel or remember or do. Let yourself go forward in freedom, and don't try too hard to figure things out. Some stories will speak to you, and you may spend much time with them. Other days, prayer may be as dry as a pot of rice left on the stove way too long. Please know that all this is normal and good. The workings of God in the soul are mysterious.

We can slog on for weeks or months, and then have a breakthrough. The secrets of our lives are hidden in plain sight, in the stuff of consolation and sadness as they come to us every day. We are like leaves that turn toward the sun, or we turn away for a time. Now, on this journey, we seek to return with open hearts. Nothing else is needed.

As you review your prayers for the week, remember that nothing is lost; no prayer is done without reward. As you review your spiritual checkup, don't take interpretations too far, but don't be afraid to explore either. Stay close to your inner truth and the ordinary stuff of life as you allow your mind to soar. Go gently, and love yourself.

Extra Thought for the Day...
Life itself is like gumbo, too. It is a tasty dish filled with many good things. Learn to take time to really taste life, without constantly thinking about, "the next thing." Practice being in the moment, being present, "now." A good way to do this is to find some things that bring you pleasure, little things you enjoy doing.

Activities
You may want to treat yourself to one of these activities today, or in the days to come.

+ Take a slow, easy walk, regardless of the weather, and relish the beauty that exists in every season.
+ Take special notice of the people being placed in your path and take time to enjoy them.
+ Read inspiring poetry, like that of Gerard Manley Hopkins or Emily Dickinson.
+ Have a conversation with a good and trusted friend about the journey you are on spiritually. (Don't pick an "advice giver.")

+ Listen to some classical music, or really good jazz or blues.
+ Make a cake from scratch and share it with some friends or bake and decorate cookies for the season.
+ Take a wonderful, scented bath with candles burning.
+ Watch an inspiring movie. (These are often the old ones.)
+ Play a pickup game of basketball.
+ Read an inspiring biography.

FOR REFLECTION AND JOURNALING

+ Review your journaling for the week. Using a highlighter, emphasize times that you felt yourself moving forward in this process.

CLOSING PRAYER

The angel says,
"Get up and eat,
Get up and eat my friend,
Or the journey will be too long for you."
Nourish your body, your mind and your soul
With beauty and love and the good things of the earth.
Enjoy your life before it is too late.

Week Three

LOOKING ABOUT: FINDING MY LIFE NOW

We made a plan for daily prayer.
We took our spiritual temperature,
Began to look within our hearts.
In certain little ways, light is dawning.
God is walking with us daily.
Now we look at our daily lives.
God has put us in a certain place,
With unique tasks to do,
And specific people who are in our lives.
What do these people and tasks teach us about our spiritual lives ?
What are we drawn to see and discover in the stuff of every day life?
Where are our wounds driving us?
What nourishes God within us?
What calls out for change?

Week Three: Day One

FAMILY: JOY AND PAIN

I love you, O LORD, my strength.
The LORD is my rock, my fortress, and my deliverer....
—Psalm 18:1–2

Come now, take heart. These days are very meritous
for gaining heaven.
—Teresa of Avila

I believe that the spiritual life is lived in the every day. As you look about your life today, begin to embrace the belief that there is no division between things that are spiritual and non-spiritual. As we live out our Christian, incarnate spirituality, healing comes in our embracing love and surrender.

I always laugh ruefully and call interaction with family the graduate school of spirituality. Our families, the ones from which we came and those we help create, are often the source of our richest joy and our most heartfelt struggle.

I had just plugged the coffee pot in this morning when the phone rang. It was Marie, a close friend whom I had shepherded through the Nineteenth Annotation retreat of Saint Ignatius. This meant that we had met together for a year, and she had shared deeply from her heart all the challenges and gifts that came to her from a very large extended family, most of whom live near her. She has taught me more than I have ever taught her.

This morning she related her ongoing struggle with her elderly mother-in-law, who lives with Marie and had suffered the loss of two children and her husband. Yet she has other children and numerous grandchildren who love her and give her much attention. Nothing seems to satisfy, however, and Marie bears the brunt of the lady's growing dissatisfaction over her declining health and circumstances. Marie struggles daily with speaking her truth or stuffing it, with showering her mother-in-law with love and patience while at the same time setting boundaries. Marie has developed health problems herself and has struggled with depression.

Marie told me when she called that she had just had one her hardest weeks with her mother-in-law, and that finally some other family members had stepped in on a daily basis to help. On the phone she shared tears of frustration and a growing hope that things would improve for everyone.

Many of us are caught in the sandwich generation: we are taking care of ailing parents while still trying to foster the independence of adult children. This can lead to exhaustion. Also, dealing with family makes us aware of old wounds from our past: the times we didn't get enough love, the times we were hurt. During this healing journey, embrace all of your feelings with love. Try hard not to label yourself as unworthy or evil for feeling certain things. We remember that it is never our *feelings* that are sinful, only our actions that can be. If at any time feelings threaten to become overwhelming, do seek out a compassionate listening ear. Have courage as you remember that these days are meritous for gaining heaven.

FOR REFLECTION AND JOURNALING

+ If you feel you have answered some of these questions in previous days, you may highlight those answers in your journal. However, this is core work of this process, so don't neglect it.
+ Who constitutes your family?
+ Who gives you the greatest joy? Explain.
+ Who gives you your biggest struggle? Explain.
+ Today as you pray for them and yourself, journal about

those individuals that make up your family. You may even want to sketch a small family tree. It is amazing to ponder that if, as I believe, God creates us in the particular, then he planned for these people to populate our lives. What do they have to teach us? What do we need to learn?

CLOSING PRAYER
Lord, my Rock,
my fortress, my deliverer.
Deliver me from myself!
The self that does for others what they should do for themselves.
The self that takes things personally, as much as I try not to.
Deliver me from self-pity,
let me forgive those who trespass against me.
But give me deep respect for my healing wounds,
as in you I take refuge.
and beside you, I sing for joy!
Amen.

Week Three: Day Two

SEEING MYSELF THROUGH MY SON'S EYES: THOUGHTS ON FAMILY CONTINUE

> In reality, our growth is hidden. It is accomplished by the release of our current defense postures, by the letting go of fear and our attachment to our self-image.
> —Richard Rohr, *Everything Belongs*

When my son Jacques was in high school, he had to write an autobiography. I was anxious to read it and to see how I was reflected. (That is pretty shallow, isn't it? My attitude pinches me now, years later!) I came across these words, "I get my sense of humor from my dad. My mom is a serious professional person." Gosh. I always thought I was funny, too. There went a little piece of my self-image. Looking back now, I remember that my son's high school days were difficult for me. I guess my jokes and smiles were rather scarce. Could the page shout any louder for me to *lighten up?* I often think about this incident as I take the time to enjoy a funny story or situation. I allow myself to laugh deeply and fully. It's good medicine.

Sometimes our family can make us laugh. Often they can make us cry. As Father Rohr says, we need to let go of our fear and our images of ourselves. We need to relax and know that there is more to us than what our family sees. And more to our family than what we see.

FOR REFLECTION AND JOURNALING

+ One of the gifts (and sometimes wounds) of family is that they reflect us to our own eyes. We see ourselves in them, and they interpret us in ways we don't expect. As you continue to write about your family, consider those who are similar to you in many ways.

+ What is your birth order? How has being the youngest, oldest, or in the middle affected you?

+ What traits are you known for in your family? Are you the helpful one, the funny one? Do you think this is the way you really are?

+ What image of yourself do you treasure most?

+ Do your relationships with your children help you to be a better person? Or do you think that these relationships are a challenge to your spirituality? Explain.

CLOSING PRAYER

God, let me release my defenses, if only a little.
Let my self-image not be so rigid,

My need to be *just right* not so compelling.
What my soul really wants is intimacy.
Lighten me up, God, and let me learn
To chuckle at myself
As an indulgent Mother chuckles
At her toddling babe.
Amen.

Week Three: Day Three

FINDING THE LOST PAPER CLIPS: THE CULTURAL CONSCIOUSNESS OF WORK

> You show me the path of life.
>
>> In your presence there is fullness of joy;
>>
>>> in your right hand are pleasures for evermore.
>
> —Psalm 16:11

> Reflect on any situation in your life where you are
> feeling driven. Who or what is doing the driving?
> —Margaret Silf, *Inner Compass*

A large part of assessing our lives as they are today consists of considering the work we do in the world. Some of us work in our homes, our churches, our schools. Others of us travel to offices or stores or factories. Our jobs can provide us with many good things. We can help to meet our family's needs with the money work provides. It gives us a sense of purpose and community and, in the best cases, we are truly using our God-given gifts at work.

Today, I sit all alone at a computer, yet I feel tied to you, the reader, wherever you are. Does your work fulfill you? I wonder if your work takes all your energy. I wonder if you feel defined by your work. How does it fit into your life...or does your life have to fit around it?

I was listening to a speaker several weeks ago, and I was fascinated to hear about a recent study in which ten CEOs of thriving corporations were taken to a retreat center and relieved of their laptops, cell phones, pagers and daybooks. There was no television or radio. They were left alone with themselves. The researcher reported that within two hours or less each was showing signs of grief and depression. With exterior meaning stripped away, the researcher said, they began to think about their lives beyond their work, and what they saw was not a pretty picture. There were children in trouble and marriages floundering. They lack the inner resources to be alone with themselves.

Another factor for the success-driven life is that some people develop an addiction to stress, as described by Gerald May in his book *Addiction and Grace*. When we have this addiction, we learn to function so well with lots of stress that to be without it makes us feel empty and worthless. We fall into a deep funk. Stress is our drug, and without it we cannot function. We have to detoxify from stress as from any other drug. And, when any of us have our normal distractions stripped away, whether it is stress, busyness or noise, we may be forced to deal with a deep emptiness within.

It is easy in our culture to become overly identified with *what we do to earn money*. This can become the most important thing. Our identity in other areas can become pushed back and lost. Begin to work on recovering *who you are*. You are so much more than your work.

Some of us choose to remain fully in the exterior life and get busier and busier. Many choose this path, and our culture encourages them to do so. We live in a society that values productivity and results. We pride ourselves on being too busy until our feelings rise up and surprise us.

I remember one day at work when I became obsessed with finding some colored paper clips that I had mislaid. After tearing through my office looking for them, I stopped and took stock. What was this about? Surely this was a symptom of something larger? Why was I becoming so driven? When I settled down I realized I was angry at all the paperwork that was required of me. I felt overwhelmed and frustrated by that and by many other things. Perhaps you do, too. Some things we can change. Some things we can, with God's help, learn to cope with gracefully, without a great cost to our health and happiness.

FOR REFLECTION AND JOURNALING

+ Write a few sentences about your life at work. What are the gifts of your work? Is stress driving your life? Perhaps you are different. Perhaps being *too* busy is a temptation you have already vanquished. Or perhaps stress at work is a major reason that you long for peace and clarification on this prayer journey. In any case, God is with you— loving you, helping you, sustaining you.

+ Look at the aspects of your work life that you may be able to control, and those aspects that you have to live with. Don't limit yourself, though. Many times when I direct people, I sense that it is their own need that keeps them overworked and anxious. It may be the need to be needed or valued above others. It may be the desire to acquire material things that really aren't necessary. In this culture, we all tend to do this! Be alert and watchful as you look at your life at work.

CLOSING PRAYER

Well, Lord, now we are in the journey, deeply, together. Work is hard, and work is life. Work is so many things. Didn't you give me this work to do?

Work with me today. Let me work with awareness, slowly
and carefully,
Quick reactions and decisions are not your will. But a heart
open to love always is.
Let me love myself and others more today,
And accept the very stuff of my life at work. Amen.

Week Three: Day Four

THE GRIND OF SCHEDULE, THE HOPE FOR CHANGE

As she struggles to establish a campsite for her vision
quest, author Paula D'Arcy writes,

> Aren't I feeling, with every footstep, what every man
> and woman feels when they are called on to achingly
> repeat the same tasks day after day?... I am the
> migrant worker in the fields, picking beans, or the
> teacher repeating the same lesson while few pay
> attention.... I am on the assembly line, or a parent
> getting up in the middle of the night for a crying child.
> The same task, again. And again. In my bones and in
> my blisters I feel the weight of obedience to the
> sameness which is unavoidable in all our lives.
> —Paula D'Arcy, *Gift of the Red Bird*

As we look around our lives today we consider your busyness and mine. We take up our schedules as though they
were the Holy Grail. They tell us about where our hearts
are and what our treasure is.

What is your daily schedule like? What is the purpose of
your scheduled time? Do you allow yourself a schedule that
gives you time to be? To have an inner life? To heal, rest and
live in gratitude? Has the sameness of your tasks caused
you to become somewhat numb in daily life?

In the book *The Holy Way,* author Paula Huston fully commits herself to a life of simplicity and prayer. She is told by her spiritual director to cut her commitments in half. She struggles to do this, as she realizes that she can't have it all. She can't have a life of simplicity and prayer and try to do everything else, too. Told by the same director to cut her commitments in half again, she encounters painful surrender and loss of identity in a deep and painful way.

Paula D'Arcy continues her camping meditation in this way: "Suddenly I feel the love God has for all people as we live our insignificant lives and perform our routine tasks.... I see how God honors simple obedience to our smallest tasks."[3]

FOR REFLECTION AND JOURNALING

+ Does your schedule reflect where your heart is?
+ Does meaning lie in what you do, or the way in which you do it?
+ Does love order your steps?
+ Are you obedient to your inner voice in your tasks?
+ Take a look at your daily and weekly schedule. So many things and people in our lives pull and tug on us. One thing that makes this difficult is that we are often choosing between the good and the good. How do we know what to do? In discernment we look at those areas of our lives that are within our control and those commitments that are not voluntary. If we really look with honesty at everything, our insights may surprise us. Are we trying too hard to have it all? To please everyone? And are we allowing that which we do to be imbued with love?

CLOSING PRAYER

Take the pencil in your hand, God, or the little stylus,
Take up my calendar, my appointment book, my PDA.

What are you scratching out?
What are you smiling at?
Let me see...Oh, my goodness,
I didn't expect this...the ways you look at my life,
And see what matters and what does not. Amen.

Week Three: Day Five

LOVE'S SACRED FACE: SEEING GOD IN COMMUNITY

> People you'd normally find handling cash registers or
> fixing jammed drains or coaching soccer were all on
> their knees, waiting with great hope to be healed and
> forgiven.
> —Paula Huston, *The Holy Way*

As we look at our lives as they are today, we consider our communities of faith.

Yesterday I attended Mass at St. Joseph's, my local parish. With all apologies to Father Keith, my sermon for the day came from nearby worshippers. The first was a father who tenderly cradled a girl child of about three months of age in his arms. The baby was just at an age where infants begin to wake a little to the world, to look around a bit. She was perfectly content and calm in her tiny, lime green dress, held in her dad's embrace.

The father could not have been more tender, constantly kissing the top of her little head and lifting and turning her to keep her amused. Sometimes he faced her toward him and looked into her eyes. She gazed at him, transfixed. Oh, the sweet dance they danced, the grace of it.

The second part of my sermon came during the Our Father. I knew the retired teacher sitting next to me. She was not able to kneel or constantly stand, so she sat quiet and still in her pew during all our ups and downs. During the Our Father, however, she made a painful effort and rose to her feet. She gave me her hand. It was bent and swollen, twisted with arthritis, locked into an unnatural position. What humility (or was it the longing for touch?) I saw as she gave me her hand. The part of the liturgy in which we joined in this way held the highest significance for her. Did she see Christ in me? I saw Christ in her, and in the young father, all tenderness and love.

Lost in love with his child, the young father was outside the confines of ego. He was one in love with the baby, all service to her, the helpless one. The retired teacher had a large heart, not one that locked her in pride and denial of her pain. She transcended ego when she reached out to touch and be touched, when she united her suffering with others, with liturgy, with Christ. I saw in both beautiful tableaux the face of God and love. My ego was muted as my love merged with theirs. I felt the embrace of community. This was truly worship for me. I found the love that wants to express itself in me and is reflected in the faces of those around me—my worshipping community

For Reflection and Journaling

+ What is church or spiritual home for you? Where do you worship or communicate in freedom and love? Is there struggle in this area for you?
+ Do you find your own longing for unity reflected in those around you? Name those who pray with you.
+ What friends in your life allow you to see the best in yourself?

Closing Prayer

People continually come into my life at just the right moment, God.

Some come to teach, others to comfort, some to challenge....
People come in all sorts of packages....Some smile a lot,
and others are serious.
They bring me back to laughter, and help me regain my per-
spective.
Thank you for people, Lord.
Amen.
—adapted from Joyce Rupp, *The Cosmic Dance*

Week Three: Day Six

I Long for You, O Lord: Moving to Consolation

> The issue is not whether a woman can achieve, but
> that preoccupation with achievement may deny a
> descent into her deeper nature which a woman must
> make to touch her true strengths.
> —Judith Duerk, *Circle of Stones*

As we continue to look around our lives today, we think
about those things that bring us consolation and those circumstances and even people that lead us more into desolation. God moves and works through both our consolation
and desolation. Explained simply, consolation is peace of
mind and heart that draws us closer to God. Desolation is
darkness and destructive inner voices that drive us farther
from God.

When we experience consolation, it is often because our
actions are in line with our inner desires. My friend Robin
says it this way, "God is speaking through our core
desires."

In the days before I retired from teaching, my desire to
leave my work at school deepened and deepened. My other
life, as I called it, a life of spiritual work, was taking over my
heart and my energy. I had been able to at least partially

descend into my deeper nature and access my core desires. I was in consolation when I was working in my core-desire area: giving retreats, learning new things about spirituality and writing. Desolation began to haunt my steps at school.

By the time I left the world of childhood education, I had little to give to it. I was fortunate that I could retire. Many don't have these easy options.

But there are things we can control; aspects of our time and our commitments that we can change. We may be hooked on the feeling of being needed, or on achievement as our culture sees it. Perhaps we say, "No one can do this as we do." And yet, just as I saw when I left teaching, no one is indispensable. People will carry on without us quite well, if we leave where we are not supposed to be.

One man found that his true vocation was simply to be more appreciative of others. He began to practice his core desire, while changing little about his exterior life.

FOR REFLECTION AND JOURNALING

+ What are the longings of your heart today?

+ What is your core desire?

+ If this feels like a call to spend more time in prayer and less time in busyness and doing, honor that call, that longing within your soul. Descending into your deeper nature is necessary to access the heart of your longings. It may not be easy at first; you will struggle with unknowing and discomfort. But it will be such a worthy undertaking for you; the reward will be so great.

CLOSING PRAYER

O sing to the LORD a new song;
　　sing to the LORD, all the earth.
Sing to the LORD, bless his name. (Psalm 96:1–2)

Show me the places my heart can sing your praises, my God.
Show me the ways I can fully bless your name.
Amen.

Week Three: Day Seven

Rejoicing in the Gift: Looking Around at Blessings

> Happy are those who find wisdom,
>> and those who get understanding,
> for her income is better than silver,
>> and her revenue better than gold.
> —Proverbs 3:13–14

It is said so often as to sound trite, but I cannot help but think about this: We in America are very, very fortunate people. The safety, peace, (despite recent turmoil), the health care, information and the material goods that we have access to are truly amazing, as is our freedom of speech and religion. This shower of blessings does not make us better, wiser or kinder than people in other countries, of course! But thinking about our blessings can open our hearts to compassion for all the world.

I had many reasons to think about blessings today. There is a first frost on the ground today; we call it south Louisiana snow, and the windows of my little porch are frosted over. The sunlight comes in diffuse and watery, more white than yellow. It was a struggle to get out of my warm bed (Dee's still there; he worked late last night), and it is a fumble-bumble to make the coffee. But as it perks I am filled with a secret joy: I get to go write all day long! Wow! What a gift. It is a gift that I wouldn't have thought possible ten years ago. And I am enjoying writing this book today, because I visualize you reading it and connecting with me and the Spirit in a circle dance of healing and joy. This is a core desire of my heart, brought by a wisdom that is far greater than I am. It brings a yield far better than gold.

FOR REFLECTION AND JOURNALING

+ What do you count as your blessings? Explain.
+ How is your daily work impacting your life? What core desire is calling to you?
+ What changes in your daily life would you like to instigate?
+ In general, what are your thoughts and your feelings today?

CLOSING PRAYER

Spirit of my heart,
Fear and joy jump within me when I consider the longings of my heart.
I desire to serve Love—in the freedom of life's dance.
Take my hands and dance with me, too!
Your healing is gentle and not forced.
We dance the circle dance of love and joy!
While fear just looks on, but does not join.
Amen.

Week Four

LOOKING BACK: THE LIFELINE

Slowly, we have found our place in prayer.
We have looked at inner and outer landscapes as they are
in the present,
And explored our work, our family, our community—
The whisper of longings within.
Now we look back with gentle love and care
At the lifeline journey, unfolding since our birth.
Slowly remembering that everything we are,
And everything we do,
Has been gifted to us,
By the joys and wounds of our lives,
And those who have loved us,
Early and late.

Week Four: Day One

FINDING YOUR STORY

> The plot of your life is the central story of your life, the
> main narrative strand. That strand of narrative is
> moved along by stepping-stones, or "landmark events"...
> The more you remember the landmark events in your
> life, the clearer the plot and the linkage between the
> events become. Your journal can become that place
> where you discover your stories. You tell your stories
> not only to yourself in your journal, but also to God.
> —Eddie Ensley and Robert Herrmann, *Writing to Be
> Whole*

PLOTTING MY LIFELINE

The socialization process of children, even done with the best
of intentions and the most compassionate of efforts, seems to
leave wounds and scars. Often those doing the socialization
(or child-rearing) are wounded and confused themselves,
causing the ill effects to intensify. Our schools, with their
need to educate the masses, often trample upon the tender
feelings and fledgling hopes of the individual child.

Many, even most, people have basic, longstanding
wounds that still call out for healing. These wounds usually
relate to family of origin issues: relationships with parents
and siblings. Other wounds layer over these original scars
as the person goes through life: disappointments and scars
that come from school, friendships (betrayals), and career
and marriage difficulties. Often a person learns ways of
coping that ensure survival in the family, but serve him or
her poorly in adult life.

Mental health professionals have labeled one cluster of
these behaviors as codependency. In this affliction, the per-

son loses track of his true emotions and goals, as he lives to please another and prevent anger or pain in that other. As we look at these issues, we affirm that the family tree is variegated; it bears fruit both bitter and sweet.

The contemplative monk Thomas Keating says it this way: "We have to entrust the whole tree, root, trunk and branches, to the mercy of God who alone can heal the radical distortion of the human condition."[4] This is the deep conversion that we seek.

Keating says that much of our mistaken behavior springs from a false self, and makes us seek our own ends by hook or crook and strive to keep ourselves powerful and comfortable at the expense of others. Living out of the false self leads us to create drama and pain in our lives. We can become victims or martyrs, or both. Richard Rohr agrees, and says that conversion is, "the healing of the false self, the redemption of the authentic self."

FOR REFLECTION AND JOURNALING

+ During this week you will construct a lifeline with landmark events written down. The purpose of this lifeline is to discover the ways events have affected you in your life and the ways that God has been with you throughout all your life.
+ Take some pieces of blank paper and draw your lifeline. Do this by drawing a straight line down the middle of the paper. Then intersect the line with perpendicular lines. These intersecting lines will represent ten-year intervals in your life. (You may want to use shorter intervals for your early childhood.) Write on these perpendicular lines the major things that happened in your life: *I was born. My little brother was born; we moved to a new town. Dad lost his job. I had measles for four weeks. I made my confirmation. I made the dance team. (You know, I still love to*

dance, even today.) My mother was very ill for two years. I went off to college; I didn't make good enough grades and so I went into the service, went to France, married Sally. My son Christopher was born. I was made vice president of sales....My father died, and so on.

+ This is your task for the week. You don't have just today to do this, so take your time. Also begin to journal and pray with the memories that surface for you.

CLOSING PRAYER

The LORD is my shepherd, I shall not want.

  He makes me lie down in green pastures;
he leads me beside still waters;

  he restores my soul.

—Psalm 23:1–3

Week Four: Day Two

THE RABBIT ROAD

> And where was God in all of this? What are my remembrances of God's presence? Who has God been for me in all the ages of my life? How have my images of God changed over the years? Quieting my mind, I recall the God who has journeyed with me through childhood, on into adolescence and into my young adult years.
>
> —Macrina Wiederkehr, *Behold Your Life*

Charting your lifeline may bring up many memories for you. This one surfaced for me recently, and I enjoyed reliving a magic moment of childhood.

It is a summer morning and I am seven or eight years old. I slam out of the large, wooden farmhouse and run to the Rabbit Road. Up the driveway past the orchard, through the place we call the lot, where barns and farm equipment stand, and into a little lane, bordered by an overgrown fence line. I run down the little byway and into another world.

I don't remember how long this magic lane was, but I felt so removed there as I crushed up berries to make ink and fashioned a floor plan out of castaway bricks, building a little home for me and my imaginary family. I felt sheltered and contained, yet free. Often my latest puppy would run with me. I would spend whole summer days on the Rabbit Road. No one worried about me; I was safe on a country lane far from town. I guess I returned home when I got hungry. Life was simple and magical here, filled with the possibilities of endless summer days.

Here my sensitive spirit could rest and just *be*. There were no demands here, no stresses. God was raising a small and gentle soul as a small girl played on the Rabbit Road.

FOR REFLECTION AND JOURNALING

+ Continue to work on your lifeline. In your life story is the heart of your being. Did you have a favorite hideout or a loved activity when you were a child? Who were your playmates, your pets? Use some color now. You may want to draw some stick figures, or color events red-letter days or blue days. There is no right or wrong way to do this. Experiment. Use more sheets of paper as needed.

+ Enjoy your lifeline. Cherish it! As you revisit the experiences, try to remember the feeling quality of them. Be kind to yourself as you look at everything.

CLOSING PRAYER

You laid a table before me
You filled it with good things.
Crushed berries on a summer's day,
A popsicle and watermelon.
Back when the sun was warm and days were endless.
But on some of your small ones, the sun shone faintly,
if at all.
So for all those on this journey with me,
Those clearly blessed, those with sad and hidden faces,
For everyone, for each one, I pray.
I pray.
Amen.

Week Four: Day Three

ON THE PLAYGROUND

> Whenever you feel lonely, you must try to find the
> source of this feeling. You are inclined either to run
> away from your loneliness or to dwell in it.... This
> identification is not an intellectual task; it is a task of
> the heart. ...Your loneliness may be revealed to you as
> the other side of your unique gift.
> —Henri Nouwen, *The Inner Voice of Love*

As you continue your lifeline, you will encounter the memories of school years. This is one of my most painful ones.

When I was in the middle of my first grade year, my
family moved. I left a small, friendly country school where
I was given much attention, and entered a much larger
town school in the middle of a cold, bleak winter. I was truly
miserable. My mother recalls that each night I would cry
and beg her not to send me to school the next day.

My teacher in the new school was young, and she wasn't very patient with small children. I felt a deep homesickness for my old teacher and a feeling of not being accepted. I would often stand alone on the cold playground and watch others play.

My mother remembers going to school and asking the teacher to give me a job like dusting, so that I would feel included. I don't remember this part of the story, but as time passed, I adjusted. By the middle of second grade at the same school, I loved my teacher, had friends, and was doing well.

I wonder now if God looked with compassion upon a thin little girl pressed against a brick wall, hiding from a cold winter wind. I believe God did. And on some days when I am feeling lonely, I might need to comfort the shivering little girl who waits alone for a friend to ask her to play.

FOR REFLECTION AND JOURNALING

+ Continue your lifeline work.
+ What were your school years like? Were you good at academics? Did you have friends?
+ If you went to a religious school, how did that shape your early years?
+ Do you recall any specific major events at this time? A move? The birth of a new brother or sister? A change in your parents' work or lives? Explain.
+ Are there specific ways that you remember God's presence at that time?

CLOSING PRAYER

You led me through valleys of shadows,
where cold winds blew and fingers numbed.
You led me to greener pastures, beside water that reflected my joy.

Surely you have always been with me.
Always, you have been with me.
Amen.
—adapted from Psalm 23

Week Four: Day Four

CHILDHOOD WOUNDS

> In you O LORD, I take refuge;
>
> let me never be put to shame.
>
> —Psalm 71:1

We are most vulnerable to wounds to our hearts during our childhood. Psychologists tell us that these wounds can be the hardest to overcome and to heal. This story illustrates one such wounding occasion that happened to a friend of mine.

Violet was thirteen years old and was happily singing in the school choir. One day the group was rehearsing for a special concert. The music teacher, Mrs. Sanford, directed the group with a puzzled expression on her face. Then she zeroed in on Violet.

"Violet, my dear, you are a whole note off pitch! Well, we can't correct that in time for the concert. Just move your lips, dear, but don't sing." Violet remained for the practice, fighting tears, but she quit the choir before the concert.

Violet is now fifty-four, but she won't sing in public. Actually, she doesn't even sing in the shower. The public rebuke about her voice, when she was too young to fight back or to process the information, left a permanent wound within her. Deep toxic shame related to this issue entered her heart.

Many of us have stories like this. I wasn't good at all at *group* sports when I was growing up. (Well, I still am not!)

But one day I was remarking to a friend that I *just wasn't athletic*. She surprised me by saying, "You are one of the most athletic people I know! You're always walking or biking or swimming. Where did you get the idea you weren't athletic?"

My friend's comments helped me to recast my ideas about myself. I couldn't make a goal in basketball, but I could use and enjoy my body in an active way. This was healing for me. Maybe I wasn't such a klutz after all.

FOR REFLECTION AND JOURNALING

+ Take some time now to begin to examine some of your wounds. Remember Jesus is with you. Give a friend or other members of your spiritual group a call if you feel the need to talk anything out. If you know you were, or may have been, a victim of abuse in childhood and you are still very wounded from these incidents, you may want to skip this exercise or do things like this with a therapist or other professional. For many of us, though, it will be an enlightening trip back.

+ Continue to work on your lifeline.

+ What were your strengths when you were young? Your talents?

+ Can you recall any incidents when you were young when your talents or gifts were discounted, or where you felt inadequate?

A MEDITATION FOR THE HEALING OF CHILDHOOD WOUNDS

(Note: If you have had traumatic experiences in your childhood, such as severe abuse, especially if you have not received help for them, you will probably not want to do this meditation, or you may need a friend or health professional present. This meditation is for the normal wounds of childhood that most people experience.)

You will need at least twenty minutes in a private place. In fantasy, take yourself back to an event of wounding or shaming in your childhood. Place yourself in the scene as an adult, observing the child that you were. Take Jesus with you. See the face of Jesus clearly: How is he dressed? What is his coloring, his appearance? Spend some time visualizing all of this: sights, colors, sounds, even smells.

Then, as the adult you are now, go to the child with Jesus beside you. You may want to rescue the child that you were from the event or comfort her or him. You can also visualize the child taking up for herself or himself and confronting the wrongdoer. You and Jesus will take turns holding the child you were in your arms. Both of you will speak words of love, affirmation and hope.

Repeat this exercise as often, and as with as many events, as desired.

CLOSING PRAYER

Happy are those who consider the poor;
    the LORD delivers them in the day of trouble
The LORD protects them and keeps them alive;
    they are called happy in the land.
Amen.
—from Psalm 41:1–2

Week Four: Day Five

SYMBOLS OF DEATH AND LOSS

> I will need to wait the darkness out; say it out, pray it out.
>
> —Joyce Rupp, *The Star in My Heart*

Tracing our lifeline and revisiting our past will inevitably bring us face to face with loss.

I heard one such poignant story around the breakfast table at Our Lady of the Oaks in Grand Coteau, Louisiana:

> Laurie was fourteen years old and was skating on the sidewalk in front of her house. She wore the type of skate that clips onto a shoe and is tightened with a key. Suddenly her father appeared beside her. He stopped her and folded her into a gentle embrace. Through tears he told her that her ill mother had just passed away.
>
> Many years later, Laurie discovered the skate key in a box of almost-forgotten mementos. Bittersweet feelings swept over her. She remembered a carefree day of youth that had been crushed with aching loss. She held the key in her hand and pondered it for many minutes. She later placed it in her jewelry box.
>
> A few years later Laurie's church parish planned a new worship space. An artist designed massive bronze doors for the entrance of the new church. He made a wax cast of the doors and invited the members of the parish to press important objects of remembrance into the wax. When the objects were removed, an impression was made that would later be revealed on the finished doors.
>
> Laurie took the skate key and pressed it into the wax cast. Now each time she enters her worship space she can remember her mother with love and gratitude. Time has softened the pain of memory and has allowed the gentle, happy times with her mother to fill her heart, even though the feeling of loss remains. She experiences a richness of emotion, colored by love.

For Reflection and Journaling

+ Whose death or absence has made an impact upon your life? Journal and reflect about this. What symbols are important to you? Explain.

Closing Prayer

I waited patiently for the LORD;
    he inclined to me and heard my cry.
He drew me up from the desolate pit,
    out of the miry bog,
and set my feet upon a rock,
    making my steps secure.
He put a new song in my mouth,
    a song of praise to our God.
He pulled me up
He set my feet on the rock,
And made my footsteps firm.
He put a fresh song in my mouth.
I am poor and needy,
    but the Lord takes thought for me.
You are my help and my deliverer;
    do not delay, O my God.
—adapted from Psalm 40:1–3

Week Four: Day Six

Our Parents: Like Big Fish?

> But we need the wisdom of the ages, too. We can't start at zero.
>
> —Richard Rohr, *Everything Belongs*

In the entertaining and mystical movie *Big Fish,* a son struggles to understand his father and his father's life. The father is a tall-tale-teller, and the son is frustrated as he tries to separate fact from fiction. This is a father who always had to be heroic and larger than life. His tales hid his vulnerability and even his love, while at the same time revealing them in language not always understood.

I related to this movie because my dad so loves a good story, although he doesn't try to make himself bigger in stories. He often pokes fun at himself, and I often tell stories that are self-deprecating also. Perhaps Dad is one reason I write today; in fact, he surely is. My dad's humor got him through dark days. He is a gregarious, people-person whom others like automatically. I cherish the part of my personality that is like his.

My parents grew up in another time and were influenced by another set of cultural rules than I. People were not encouraged to share their pain, but to be strong and to carry on. When I consider that my parents lived through both a depression and a major world war, I know they needed these tools of strength. My mother was and is such a hard worker. She had to be, to care for four children and teach full-time while caring for a home and a farm. (Just at this very moment, as I write this, I see the pattern: *my* mom was a serious professional person.)

And from my mother I get my love of the written and spoken word, my delight in flowers, my attention to the clothes I wear. She's a great experimental cook, and I tend to excel in that area also. You may want to notice your similarities with and differences from your parents or other caregivers as you do this deeply spiritual work you are doing now.

For it is through our parents and grandparents that we have the opportunity to access the wisdom of the ages. But parents bring their own human brokenness to our lives as well.

Many of our parents were driven by work and sometimes by the need to just survive and provide for a family. They were also shaped by their desires for their children to have an easier life than they did.

Other parents were lost in addictions or their own wounds. Some used religion like a weapon; some seemed to know little about what children need.

Still other parents created a magical and safe and place for their children to flourish. All of the traits of our parents and caregivers have helped to form us into the people we are today. And now we look at them and ourselves with compassion.

FOR REFLECTION AND JOURNALING

+ What were your parents like? Write a short paragraph about each of them and the traits you share with them or your differences.

CLOSING PRAYER

Can you bless your parents today and pray for them? You may or may not be able to do this. Perhaps you need more to pray for yourself as you consider your parents. Spend some time doing what you need to do, and offering it all to God. Always treat yourself with love, patience and compassion.

Week Four: Day Seven

WHERE IS GOD IN ALL THIS?

> In my young adult life the gnawing ache for love
> continues. However, sometimes the drive for success
> and my competitive spirit hide my vulnerability. But
> when no one is watching it comes and stands before me
> like a sentinel bearing a silent message.
> —Macrina Wiederkehr, *Behold Your Life*

The LORD is my light and my salvation;
　　whom shall I fear?
The LORD is the stronghold of my life;
　　of whom shall I be afraid?
. . .
One thing I asked of the LORD,
　　that will I seek after:
to live in the house of the LORD
　　all the days of my life,
—Psalm 27:1, 4

We have spent the week looking back over our lives and we will do more of this work in the days to come. I was thinking about my own young adult life, and I realized that during my twenties and thirties, I made decisions based on cultural consciousness and my own feelings. Fortunately, I had a strong moral consciousness. But the idea of doing what was truly in my authentic nature meant little to me. (I laugh when I remember my venture at real estate, not a good field for someone with no sense of direction. If you can't find the house, you can't sell it. Why did I do that? I know, everyone else was doing it, and I wanted to make some money too!)

The world I lived in demanded certain things from me, I felt, and I tried to live up to my obligations and the demands of relationships, jobs and society. Only as I reached the end of my middle forties did I feel an extremely strong call to discover God's will in my life, the best use of my God-given talents and my true characteristics. I wanted to be much more than my wounds or my ambition. I went deeper and deeper within. People appeared in my path to help me. My life began to change. Yahweh became more and more my light and my salvation.

As we complete our lifeline work today, consider some of the factors that aid healing in one's life:

- Acknowledging wounds with love.
- Telling one's story to a compassionate listener who will not judge or give advice.
- Writing our story for our eyes only.
- Practicing deep prayer in which we ask God to come and heal us.
- Working to accept ourselves as we are as we acknowledge that everyone is this world is both flawed and gifted.
- Becoming active in a faith community and being of service to others.

Look at your lifeline to discover once again the major milestones in your life: the times God has been close to you, the special helpers that have appeared, and the times you felt you sought God's face in vain. Surround the pain in your life with deep prayers of love. Don't push; don't rush. Things will come as they will. This is not just a matter of gaining information, but a process of opening up and gently becoming aware. What messages are you receiving now? In what ways has your life shaped you, shaped your personality and your faith story, and made you all that you are today? It's a good thing. It really is.

CLOSING PRAYER

O God, you search me and you know me,
all my ways lie open to your gaze.
When I stand and when I sit, you draw near me.
You created me and your intimacy with me astounds me!
That you love me so much and accept me as I am,
is wondrous to me. You accept all of me,
because you understand everything about me.
Amen.
—adapted from Psalm 139

Week Five

GROUNDED IN LOVE: THE PROMISES OF JOHN 15

Our outer and inner landscapes
Are becoming known to us.
We have looked about,
Looked within and looked back at our lives.
Now we must claim the most important thing—
We are children of the kingdom,
Green-growing sprouts of Jesse's tree,
Blooming branches grafted to the vine of Jesus,
Imbibing strength of spirit in every moment,
Growing larger and yet simpler within Christ's love and
care.

Week Five: Day One

TOGETHER IN CHRIST: THE PROMISES OF JOHN 15

I am the true vine
And my Father is the vinedresser.
Every branch in me that bears no fruit he will cut away,
And every branch that does bear fruit
He prunes,
To make it bear even more.
Remain in me, and I in you,
You may ask for whatever you wish,
And you will get it.
It is the glory of the Father that you bear much fruit.
You are my friends,
If you do what I command.
I no longer call you servants,
Because a servant does not know the master's business.
I call you friends, because I have made known to you
All that I have learned from my Father.
You did not choose me.
I chose you!
I commissioned you to go out,
And bear much fruit.
And remember always, *Love one another.*
—adapted from John 15

Our lifelines meet and cross, and we desire to find community, a place to be and to share. This morning as I sit at my desk, I am fresh from directing a retreat of forty-seven men from different walks of life, with varied tasks before them and home lives that range from very satisfying to almost intolerable. Some are facing divorce. Some have lost jobs. Some are mourning for children gone far astray, lost in drug use or to shadowy lifestyles filled with darkness. One man especially is on my mind this morning. Jason is in a death to life struggle with darkness, and the sin in his life might well cause him to lose his job, his family and everything dear to him.

These men are with me as I write this morning. I can see their faces, hear their voices, feel their struggles. I love them. It is *agape* love that I feel for them, and sometimes it hurts. During the retreat, in the chapel before a talk, as sometimes happens, I was pressed into prayer on my knees by unseen hands. My prayer was deep and heartfelt, "Help them, Lord. They need you so much! Help them; heal them!" The heaviness of their lives felt like a force weighing down upon me, forcing me to admit my helplessness and my need for God, which is as deep as theirs. In that moment the call to love one another was lived out in me.

FOR REFLECTION AND JOURNALING

+ When and how have you been grafted to the vine of Jesus? What is your response to this story and to the Scripture reading? Journal about this.

CLOSING PRAYER

May I seek the quiet of this day, My Savior,
to walk and pray with you.
You tell me about the green and growing vine that is you.
You speak to me of the strength that can come from you alone.
I seek to understand this mystery and to see,
how I have tried to make it all on my own,
like a tiny seed that doesn't know
about the good, good earth.
Teach me. Heal me.
Amen.

Week Five: Day Two

Cut Off From the Vine

> Those who abide in me and I in them bear much fruit,
> because apart from me you can do nothing.
> —John 15:5

One summer morning my husband, Dee, came in from the garden infuriated at *those little devils!* Those little devils, the numerous brown and white rabbits that live on our property, had not been able to reach some of the tomatoes growing high on a particular vine. So they cut through the vine with their sharp little teeth and toppled it to the ground. It was easy to munch on the ripe, juicy tomatoes then!

A child of six knows that a branch severed from the vine cannot live. And yet, we go along, trying to live lives separated from the Spirit and based on our own strengths, our own life force, not relying on each other, not counting on God's wisdom and strength. We struggle more than we need to. I have done this so often!

My friend Sylvie told me about this painful, cut-off feeling. She recalled times in her life when she felt isolated from God, self and others. She described her inner state as "at war with myself." She believes today that the mending of her soul came as a gift of grace. "Even hope," she says, "we can't manufacture it. It comes as a grace." It comes when we are able to receive it.

As I directed that group of forty-seven men, on a very rainy weekend in Grand Coteau, they would ask me: *What am I supposed to be doing? What does God want of me? Is God asking that I be a better person, more involved? I just don't know what to do.*

I would quickly tell each of the men that I didn't know his purpose. I would then gently suggest a daily prayer time, a time of being with God and listening both to God and to the inner self.

It is through our grafting onto the vine that is Jesus that we have the opportunity to turn from the false self, a self that we have carefully constructed to fit the images that the world seeks from us. Or it is the false self within us that has been told that we are unworthy or flawed beyond redemption. This false self builds masks and defenses, and manipulates others to obtain its goals. In contrast, our true self knows itself as loved unconditionally. It can make mistakes because it knows that perfection is only an illusion. Our true self can be flexible, free, not tied up in how things turn out. It is the true inner self of compassion.

We can find this true self because we know a God that wants to know us. Our immersion in the promises of John 15 can open our ears to hear and our hearts to trust. The words of Jesus can open us to our true selves.

FOR REFLECTION AND JOURNALING
+ Journal about how your prayer time has been thus far.
+ What major issues from your present or past are you dealing with now? Journal about this.
+ Do you have a perception of your true self? Your false self? Write about this.
+ What messages are you receiving in your prayer time? What connections are you feeling, if any?
+ Do you have gratitude or pain welling within you or are you just numb? Journal about your feelings.
+ Trust that everything is unfolding as it should.

CLOSING PRAYER
Breathe quietly and rest in God's love. Ask the Great Physician to heal any inner pain you are experiencing.

You may want to repeat a mantra, such as *Jesus, Abba* or *Peace.*

You do not have to say the mantra on each breath, but just use it to bring your attention back to your center. Try to relax your mind and spirit and breathe in God's love. Try to lengthen the time period you can enjoy this type of centering prayer.

Week Five: Day Three

How Hard to Love Others!

> Wasn't he a tender friend, who could let one disciple rest his head upon his bosom, and accept a kiss from another? We haven't arrived at fulfilling the most important commandment if we have not cultivated a tender, caring love for the Lord Jesus...nor have we fulfilled it if we do not cultivate the same tender, caring love for our neighbors—our friends, our brothers and sisters, our colleagues, our companions on the journey toward the reign of God in our lives and in our world.
> —M. Basil Pennington, *Seeking His Mind*

Jesus asks us to love one another, as he has loved us. As I consider this, I chuckle over the old saying, "I love humanity; it's people I can't stand."

It is those people who cut us off at the traffic light. It is those people who don't listen to us and trample our words in conversations. Don't agree with our politics or our diet plans. Refuse to give us affirmation. It is those people at work who aren't doing their share and blame their mistakes on us. It is the family members who forget us, discount us, hurt us and disappoint us.

I know about these feelings. I have a dear godchild, Marc, who has grown into his teenage years. He is a great person, handsome, active and talented, and he will do well in this life. He's got his own agenda now, and well he should! Yet I was miffed when I got a new computer and I asked Marc to come and help me set it up. He never came; his dad came. On another occasion I offered to pay Marc to help me weed some flowerbeds (he has a lawn business), but he said he wasn't good at weeding.

During Easter time, I always give Marc and his brother and sister an Easter basket, filled with things such as little flashlights and pens, candy and an occasional CD. I was feeling resentful, and I didn't want to give Marc a basket that year. (I am sure he probably wouldn't have noticed. He certainly has everything he needs and most of what he wants.)

However, *I* needed to notice that the part of me that can be petty and vindictive and have long pity parties was rising to the surface and trying to take me over. Did I give gifts out of selfish motivations? Even worse, did I only love those who met my expectations? Did I use my disapproval like a weapon? If I did, I was reacting out of a very small heart, a hardened and selfish place within me. I was a vine that had been severed from the plant, and I was withering.

Trying to chop off that unwanted part of me would not have helped. It would have retreated into the shade, grown new roots, and twined around my heart when I least expected it. I needed to love all that was within me while seeking to heal it. To say, "Yes, I *can* be like that. That *is* me." I needed to strengthen my connection to the Christ-life and feel the unconditional love of Jesus.

I gave Marc his Easter basket, and I felt I had gained a small victory. My inner symbol for this victory is an open hand that releases and gives, doesn't hold on. It feels so good to open my hands.

As I meditate on my open hands, I feel the sap of Christ-love flowing into my heart and enlarging it once again.

FOR REFLECTION AND JOURNALING
+ Who brings out your most loving nature?
+ When are you tempted to be small, cut off from the vine?

CLOSING PRAYER
Lord, forgive me when I trespass against others,
and let my forgiveness toward them be swift and sweet.
You reward my open heart with peace, you fill my open
hands and my forgiving nature with green growth anew.
Amen.

Week Five: Day Four

GIFTED BY STRENGTH

> I become an instrument of God when I let go of my own
> need to have everything go well or to avoid failure or to
> please others or simply to make more money. I become
> God's song when I open up and trust that God's energy
> moving through me will create goodness and harmony
> through who and how I am.
> —Joyce Rupp, *May I Have This Dance?*

When we are grafted to the vine, we can practice true humility, which involves recognizing our strengths as well as our weaknesses. Although we are not God, we are asked to serve as God in the world. We can become too accustomed to reacting out of our weaknesses and in discounting our strengths. Anything that is not perfection within us is discounted. We shy away from developing new parts of ourselves.

We see our strengths only as those things pleasing to others, yet God's energy is moving within us in hidden ways, ways we don't expect. God has gifted us and calls us to see our own unique goodness. I see my talents now, and can even accept myself as a strong, competent woman. I have a heart of compassion, I am committed to inner growth. I am not perfect, yet I have learned to accept much of my shadow as part of what gives me vitality. Even my shadows are the minor chords that, when under control, add a rich harmony to the song of my life.

FOR REFLECTION AND JOURNALING

+ Consider your strengths today. Are you good at organizing? Good at writing? Showing love to others? Is working with your hands a pleasure to you? Are you one of those people persons who never meets a stranger and can get a group together easily to perform a task? Take some time to write about your strengths today, the gifts you bring to the kingdom on earth.

CLOSING PRAYER

Make no mistake about this, my dear brothers: all that is good, all that is perfect is given us from above; it come down from the Father of all light; with him there is no shadow. By his own choice he gave birth to us by the message of truth (adapted from James 1:16–18).

Dear Father of Light,
increase the light within my heart,
let me see how you have gifted me with so much!
I praise you. Amen.

Week Five: Day Five

OPENING PRAYER

Brother Jesus,
Holy Spirit,
God, Creator,
I have been journeying with you for a while now, seeking to draw closer to you.

I feel your presence and your guiding hand upon me.
Be with me still as I continue to open myself to this process
of love and prayer and healing.
Surround me now with your love and care. Amen.

LECTIO DIVINA: HOLY READING

This Benedictine method of prayer has been meaningful for
many people. Here is a process to follow to explore this
method of prayer:

Turn in your Bible to the Gospel of John, chapter fifteen.

Light a candle, and ask the Holy Spirit to come and be
with you and enlighten your heart as you read. Read a few
verses of Scripture, in this case John 15. As you read, tune
into your heart space. Stop when certain words or phrases
speak to this space within you. This is the Holy Spirit
speaking directly to you. Write these words in your journal.
Read the Scripture passage again, slowly and with an open
heart. Write any additional words or phrases down in your
journal as you desire. Meditate upon them and the message
that they bring.

FOR REFLECTION AND JOURNALING

+ Write in your journal about what God may be saying to
  you through these words. Return to them during the day
  and pray with them in the evening. Open yourself in willingness to be grafted to the vine.

CLOSING PRAYER

Jesus says to you:
I love you!
Just as the Father has loved me, I love you.
Remain in my love and never leave me.
You are my friend; I no longer call you servant.
You are a part of me, a part of my life on this earth and
forever.

Grow in peace, be deeply with me.
I give you my life, my life.
It will be new life springing up within you!
Amen.

Week Five: Day Six

REPENTANCE

> This is my commandment, that you love one another as
> I have loved you.... You are my friends if you do what I
> command you.
> —John 15:12, 14

> Repentance is the doorway to the spiritual life, the only
> way to begin. It is also the path itself; it is the only way
> to continue.
> —Frederica Mathewes-Green, *The Illumined Heart*

> Come Spirit, consuming Fire of Love,
> Fill us with enthusiasm for your vision.
> May the desire for truth be vibrant in us.
> —Joyce Rupp, *May I Have This Dance?*

We all have made poor choices and fallen away from the
highest good that God has planned for us. But especially on
this healing journey, we must approach our transgression
with compassion, the same compassion we would show
others. With this in mind, let us spend some time in repentance today. I repent of the times when:

- I didn't honor myself and God's gifts within me.
- I saw others as a means to an end and not as God's
  Beloved.
- I spent too much money on myself and didn't share. I was
  cut off from gospel values.

- I judged others and even demonized them. I enjoyed telling my friends what bad people others were. I watered and fertilized resentment and enjoyed doing it.
- I cared more about being right than about another's feelings.
- I refused to face up to my part in misunderstandings.
- I pushed someone to the margins of society.
- I was cold or uncaring; I turned away from another's pain or gave them only clichés for comfort.
- I took control; I took the spotlight; I took the highest chair.
- I saw evil, but I didn't let myself speak up.
- I became cynical and spent, with no desire to move out of my condition.
- I refused, out of fear, to get involved when I could have helped.
- I just forgot about people who needed me to say even a word, send a card, or make a call. I was too busy.

Do we really *see* those who cross our paths? Do we really know that they are children of God? Do we remember that the clerk at the store has a soul? That the lady with too many items in the express lane is someone's much-loved daughter? Do we understand that all those pushed to the fringes of our society may be getting into the kingdom before us?

It requires waking up to see this. It requires the release of the ego and the flourishing of the soul. It asks for a deeper love of self. We have to stop clinging so hard to that which we have always known and understood. It's not easy, but we are making progress. As author Julia Cameron says:

> The shift to spiritual dependency is a gradual one. We
> have been making this shift slowly and surely. With

each day we become more true to ourselves, more open to the positive.... We find we are able to tell more of our truth, hear more of other's people's truth, and encompass a far more kindly attitude toward both. We are becoming less judgmental of ourselves and others.[5]

Ah, so proceed with caution my friends. Repent, but don't beat yourself up. Love yourself as you strive to love others. I can tell you from experience; it's really the only way.

FOR REFLECTION AND JOURNALING

+ Which of the listed failings most resonated with you? Journal about this.
+ How do you feel about seeking to love others, especially strangers?
+ How did you respond to the Julia Cameron quote?
+ This may be a time to seek out the sacrament of reconciliation.

CLOSING PRAYER

Glory Be to the Father
and to the Son
and to God's Spirit within us and
around us.
as you were in the beginning, God,
so you still are: All present, all loving,
unending. Amen.

Week Five: Day Seven

GRAFTED TO THE VINE: GIVING AND RECEIVING COMPASSION

There are two ways of thinking about church and religion. One is that we go to church in order to be in the presence of the holy, to learn and to have our lives

> influenced by that presence. The other is that church
> teaches us directly and symbolically to see the sacred
> dimension in everyday life.
> —Thomas Moore, *Care of the Soul*

I just took a long walk in the nippy air, and two gentlemen at separate times stopped and asked if I needed a ride. Fortunately, they were neighbors, and I live in a neighborhood that is safe enough so that I didn't fear shady intentions from them. In fact, I was warmed by their concern. "You looked cold; that's why I stopped," said one man, pausing in his shiny moss-green SUV and speaking out of his rolled-down window.

Don't worry. I don't get into cars with people I don't know well, but their concerns made me feel grafted to the vine of community. Supported. Looked after. It is a feeling sorely missing from many folks' lives. And so, paradoxically, we must give what we want to receive. We must offer community to others in order to fill our own hearts with it. In this way the sacred enters the everyday dimension of our lives.

FOR REFLECTION AND JOURNALING

God begins to heal and call me and
I am more firmly grafted to the vine...
As unconscious actions and motivations are brought to consciousness
As I accept and cradle gently my darkness, as well as my light
As I heal my image of God
As I offer the gifts of community to others
As I realize that my actions are neither wonderful nor terrible, and it is all right
As I learn to seek God's face, to rest and to reveal myself to

God in prayer
As I trust others with my inner truth
As I write down my deepest thoughts and feelings
As I get in touch with what I need in my life
As I heal and forgive my past
As I learn whom I need to forgive
As I forgive and accept myself for not being perfect or living up to my own expectations
As I gain trust and courage through Jesus

FOR REFLECTION AND JOURNALING

+ Look over your journal for the week.
+ What does the vine image say to you? Is God the Healer becoming present?
+ What themes are emerging in your writing?

CLOSING PRAYER

Loving God, hold me in your care.
Pour the warm water of your healing over me,
Your light helps me to see the truth,
That my life unfolds in your community,
That I am a leafy branch on your vine,
That we all need grounding in your soil
Your water refreshes my spirit. Amen.

Week Six

GROUNDED IN SPIRIT: OUR IMAGES OF GOD

We are giving our hearts the attention they need.
We have experienced our grafting onto the vine that is
Jesus.
He accepts us with all our weaknesses and sins.
He celebrates our strengths, and we strive to do the same.
Now we explore in depth
Our images of God.
We seek to uncover the attitudes that keep us
From being close to God and from casting all our care and
worries
Upon the Spirit of Unconditional Love.

Week Six: Day One

SOPHIE'S VISION

> I have loved you, with an everlasting love, I have called
> you and you are mine...
> —Michael Joncas, *Glory and Praise*

> We are made human by the love affair.... We are
> challenged with the possibilities of even greater being,
> and so we must continually move toward the future,
> becoming human in the fullest sense.
> —John J. English, *Spiritual Freedom*

> We become like the God we worship.
> —Matthew Linn, *Good Goats*

I believe that nothing is more basic to our healing walk
than a positive image of our God. We are being asked to
summon up trust and faith in the love of God, and so it is
vital to see this God as one who loves us, who longs to heal
us. Faulty images of God can delay the healing we seek.

I had been seeing Sophie, a widow in her fifties, for
about three months in spiritual direction. Sophie felt that
she had stumbled into some serious sin in her life, and even
though she had confessed this and received absolution, it
still seemed to affect her spiritual life in a negative way. Her
prayers to God were stilted and seemed to hold God at arm's
length. A typical one would be, "God, I know you want me to
be holy, and when I am perfected, I will be pleasing to you."

"Sophie," I would say, "You are pleasing to God now. God
loves you unconditionally *now*. You don't have to earn that
love, nor can you lose it.

"Lyn," she would say, looking at me quizzically, "I would
like to believe that, but I just don't."

As time passed, Sophie's attitude toward God began to soften. She worked with images of Jesus as the good shepherd and God as the mother who carries us. She was particularly attracted to Mary, the mother of Christ. She found paths to the all-forgiving God through Mary.

One afternoon when Sophie came to direction her face was transformed. She told me that she had experienced a wonderful two weeks of prayer and that God had touched her in a special way. She had typed up a synopsis of the experience that she wanted to share with me.

Earlier today I felt as if I made a connection with the healing power of your grace, my sweet and loving Jesus. I was contemplating the glorious mysteries, the descent of the Holy Spirit, when I began to reach out to you, Jesus and Mary. I felt a calm and peace begin to flow down upon me. I made a connection with grace.

It must have been the grace of mercy and love that was flowing into me. The tears that fell were a welcome release of the grief that I felt at that moment. I needed to grieve, to express it; it felt good to be able to cry. To cry for all the times I held back my true feelings. I am sensitive. There is compassion in me. I felt you drawing these feelings up to the surface of my being today. I felt joy surfacing, too, and the fear abated.

There is peace in my midst today. Your peaceful presence rested in me. Your grace won over my natural tendency to resist your urgings to my soul to be open and willing to receive all the riches you wish to share. It is all grace, Jesus. Holiness is all grace.

I felt like turning cartwheels in joy! Sophie had been changed by the love affair! Only God could have demonstrated to her so wonderfully that God's love is unconditional.

Because of grace, Sophie dared to let God come close. When she did, she tasted unity and love. I pondered her insight, "It is all grace, Jesus. Holiness is all grace."

FOR REFLECTION AND JOURNALING

+ Do you agree with Sophie that holiness is all grace? Why or why not?
+ What is your reaction to her experience?
+ Is it easy or difficult for you to believe that God loves and accepts you *now*? Explain.
+ What image of God is given in the John 15 text?
+ Describe your image of God in general terms: Forgiving? Loving? Judging? Stern?

CLOSING PRAYER

Have mercy on me, O God,
     according to your steadfast love;
according to you abundant mercy
     blot out my transgressions.

. . .

Create in me a clean heart, O God,
     and put a new and right spirit within me.
Do not cast me away from your presence,
     and do not take your holy spirit from me.
Restore to me the joy of your salvation,
     and sustain in me a willing spirit.
—Psalm 51:1, 10–12

Week Six: Day Two

GOD AND SANTA: LEARNING THE DIFFERENCE

> Why, O LORD, do you stand far off?
> —Psalm 10:1

One December when my little nephew Trey was five, his busy mother was using Santa Claus to her advantage. "You'd better pick up your toys, Trey. Santa is watching," she would say, or, "Don't hit your little sister, Trey. You know Santa doesn't like that."

One day, Santa's name was invoked a little too often.

"You'd better eat those carrots, Trey. Santa is watching."

Totally exasperated, Trey folded his arms, stamped his little foot and said, "I hate that d*** Santa Claus!"

Hmmm...

Unfortunately, sometimes we grow up with Santa Claus images of God. He is a distant, hidden figure, who gives gifts for good behavior or withholds them in punishment. When we pray and answers don't come, we think it is because we have failed and God is not pleased with us. We need to imbue our God image with more depth and mystery. Sometimes we need to stop with our *whys* and just be present to ourselves and others. Santa Claus is not the image of God that Jesus gave us. You may want to contrast this image to the Prodigal Son story in Luke 15. If ever a boy deserved coal and switches, this was the boy. And yet...

Take a few minutes today to examine your childhood experiences with God and any influence they may still be having on your own life.

FOR REFLECTION AND JOURNALING

+ Read Psalm 51 or Luke 15. Reflect upon the passage, writing down images of God that you see there.
+ Have you ever experienced a Santa Claus image of God?
+ Who taught you about God when you were a child?
+ Do you remember childhood feelings about God? Jesus? The church? Sin and punishment? Rewards for being good?

CLOSING PRAYER

God, I know that it is your will that I feel close to you. Show me your true nature, and keep my heart open to your words. I pray for the grace of knowing your unconditional love. Amen.

Week Six: Day Three

PRESENT IN ALL-BEING: AN ALL-ENCOMPASSING IMAGE OF OUR GOD

> Come now, you who say, "Today or tomorrow we will go to such and such a town and spend a year there, doing business and making money." Yet you do not even know what tomorrow will bring. What is your life? For you are a mist that appears for a little while and then vanishes. Instead you ought to say, "If the Lord wishes, we will live and do this or that."
> —James 3:13–15

My writer friend, Joan, and I were attending the Catholic Writers' Conference near Tucson, Arizona. During the week that we were there, a huge gem and mineral show was going on in the city, spreading glittering treasures across the whole of Tucson: diamonds, gold, turquoise and opals. The list of gems and minerals was endless. We were able to visit the show one day, taking the shuttle in from Picture Rocks Retreat House where we were staying. But we couldn't catch it for the return trip.

The taxi drivers we consulted seemed unsure of our destination and we couldn't remember the way back. I remembered seeing a "Desert Museum" sign near our retreat house, so armed with this scanty information, one driver, newly arrived from Mexico City, agreed to take us home.

As we traveled, my friend became increasingly concerned saying, "No, this doesn't look right. These mountains are too close!" We both became somewhat nervous and as long minutes passed, I even worried about two women alone with someone that they had never seen before.

And yet, as we traveled on, the beauty of our surroundings began to take our breath away and our fear dissolved. The thin ribbon of road we traveled looped and rose into desert hills that were being tinted rose and gold by the dying sun. The huge saguaro cacti spread their arms to be dipped by the golden rays. The horizon beyond was tinting itself velvety navy blue, especially in the places where the land dropped deep into valleys.

As we absorbed all the beauty and periodically consulted a sketchy map, our driver, Juan, began to tell us about his mother who was facing breast cancer surgery the next day. He poured out his worry to us, two friendly women who just happened to be in his cab for over an hour and a half. When we finally arrived at our destination (we made a large circle, we realized the next day) Juan was smiling and so were we. He told us to disregard the meter and pay him a flat sum, because he said, it was really his fault for not knowing his way around. I gave him a nice tip, because I felt that we had gotten an extraordinary tour of a beautiful place. All that has begun in chaos ended well. It was all very well.

Our belief and trust in God never guarantees that we will arrive at our destinations filled with beauty and smiles, or that our days will be smooth and without pain; often we don't know where we're going. But perhaps if we see our God present in *all* being, all circumstances, we can take a larger look at things. We can release our preconceived ideas of the way things *must* be. We can see the good in our circumstances even when our plans go awry. We can praise a God who brings healing out of pain, order out of chaos, joy out of the deep nights of our soul. In the midst of all our changes we can say, "All is well; all is very well."

FOR REFLECTION AND JOURNALING

+ Are you known for your propensity to control things, events, and people? Why?
+ If you had been in that taxi, how would you have reacted?
+ When do you draw closest to God and when do you most trust God?
+ If possible, explain some ways you see a good God in all things.

CLOSING PRAYER

God, I increasingly seek to trust you.
I seek to surrender my will to yours.
In the mists of my life, I seek your face.
In the valleys and hills of my journey I look to you.
Chart my course, be my driver.
Let me not say, "Only this, only that."
Let me say, "God's will be done."
Amen.

Week Six: Day Four

RIDING THE DARK HORSE: DESCENDING WITH GOD INTO MYSTERY

> Is there no balm in Gilead?
> Is there no physician there?
> —Jeremiah 8:22

Sometimes our images of God must dissolve into mystery. We try to hold to God's love when everything seems to tell us that there is no such God of love. I experienced this mystery with my friend Nora when so much that she treasured was snatched away from her.

I remember standing with Nora by the coffin in the funeral home where her sixty-six-year-old husband lay. She sobbed into another friend's arms. "I can't accept it. I wish I knew why. I can't forgive God for this."

The heart attack that took Jackson had come quickly, and he died in the hospital as doctors struggled to save his life. It was his first heart attack. A diabetic, he had worked hard to maintain appropriate sugar levels, and Nora had cooked healthy meals for him. They were a team: always together, supporting each other, enjoying children and grandchildren, still in love after thirty-two years of marriage. When they became semi-retired, they remodeled their home and bought new furniture in preparation for long days and relaxing evenings spent together and with family. Now nothing made sense; all was lost, it seemed.

There comes a time in our lives when we must stare into the face of mystery without discovering reasons or logic to the working of the universe. There comes a time when despite all our rationalizations, God seems unfair, cold, uncaring, even cruel. We cannot fit the events of our lives into any kind of reasonable religious framework. We are lost and angry and adrift in what we thought we knew, but didn't.

Relationships require honesty, and I suggest that we tell God how we feel. That we pour out our anger, our frustrations, our confusion and our bitterness. I have no other remedy. We can't tell ourselves how to feel or what to think. (You have seen the rigidity and tension in those who try to make everything fit a certain framework of thought.)

Community is desperately needed at such a time. God comes to us with all compassion through others. We as friends in Christ must not shy away from the hard reality of what others are experiencing. We must not resort to clichés, nor hesitate to meet eyes filled with confusion and pain. We must stand with those who suffer, stand in the fire of not knowing.

We can only be in the confusion and ride the dark horse that we have been given. I cling to messages from theologians that God is not aloof, that God suffers with us.

As time passes, we may find that the journey on the dark horse is not what we expected. We may even arrive at places more beautiful than we could have imagined.

FOR REFLECTION AND JOURNALING

Have there been times when you have struggled with confusion with or anger at God? Explain.

CLOSING PRAYER

With full voice I cry to the Lord;
With full voice I beseech the Lord.
Before God I pour out my complaint,
Lay bare my distress.
My spirit is faint within me...
There is no escape for me...
Listen to my cry for help,
For I am brought low.
—adapted from Psalm 142

Week Six: Day Five

WAITING FOR GOD WITH PATIENCE

> Be patient, therefore, beloved, until the coming of the Lord. The farmer waits for the precious crop from the earth, being patient with it until it receives the early and late rains. You also must be patient. Strengthen your hearts, for the coming of the Lord is near.
> —James 5:7–8

Therefore the LORD waits to be gracious to you;
    therefore he will rise up to show mercy to you.
For the LORD is a God of justice;
    blessed are all those who wait for him.
—Isaiah 30:18

As we wait for God's timing in the healing of our wounds and the answers to our prayers, we are like the farmer, tending the field. I am a farmer's daughter, and I can tell you that even with scientific advances and wonderful machines, there is often nothing a farmer can do but wait, endure, hope.

My father never wanted us children to worry about the crops, but I did. I always knew when the rain had gone on too long and the cotton was rotting in the fields. I knew also when rain was desperately needed and refused to come. And yet, the crops usually survived. The life of our farming family did not end, but went on. The balance of nature will win out, in the end, even when the outcomes are not exactly as we hope.

So today, embrace a timeless God, the God of balance, and nature, the God of justice. God often does not work as we wish, but God loves us. Jesus told us this many times, as did the prophets of old. In fact, we can see the God of love trying again and again to break through to the Israelite people with words of consolation and love. And so God is seeking after us. Seeking to be with us. Be patient when the outward eye cannot see well. Be patient in the darkness as well as the light. God's work within you will not fail.

CLOSING PRAYER
Abba Prayer
Light a candle and center your breathing. Breathe out tension and holding on. Breathe in God's peace. Continue this for a while.

On the inhale, think of the word, "Abba." On the exhale, think of the word, "Trust." Clear you heart and mind of all but these words. (Try to remain with these words for fifteen minutes or so.) Later, pray this prayer:

Father, Creator, Lord of the earth,
sometimes you paint the horizons with every rich color,
the grass ripples with amber light,
and every tiny flower sings your name.

And sometimes the forest is darkened,
and I cannot sing,
I cannot even pray.
Yet still you are present in each living thing.
Let faith, not sight, inform my heart.

Lord Jesus, Brother,
your love banishes our night,
our fears and imaginings, our sorrows,
as surely as the rising sun brings us a new day.

Holy Spirit, joy of the universe,
you are mother to us,
breathing life into us.
Heal my wounds, my notions of God that are not godly,
for you invigorate us, call us to live and work in you.
Now sustain us in our sorrow,
rejoice in our rejoicing.
and hold us in your care,
as we live this day with you, and for you. Amen.

Week Six: Day Six

SAINT IGNATIUS AND HIS CHANGING IMAGE OF GOD

> Take, Lord, all my freedom. Accept all my memory,
> intellect and will. All that I have or possess, You have
> given to me; all I give back to You, and give up then to
> be governed by Your will. Grant me only the grace to
> love You, and I am sufficiently rich so that I do not ask
> for anything else.
>
> —Ignatius of Loyola, *The Spiritual Exercises*

A week ago I stood before a group of teachers from the Lake
Charles Louisiana diocese to deliver a talk on Ignatian spirituality. I told them that had you asked me what course my
life would take, when I was twenty-five or so, it would have
never included such a scenario! I was born and raised a
Methodist, and knew nothing about saints, other than the
ones in the Bible. Nor do I think I would have been
attracted to this particular one: a Basque soldier, a knight,
born in the late fourteen hundreds—an odd choice for a sensitive twentieth-century woman. Well, maybe not.

For I believe the saint was chosen *for* me in a series of
pathways in my life that led to my training in Ignatian spirituality for three years. During this time, I learned about a
man who frolicked in royal courts in his youth, fought
valiant battles (sometimes in a very unadvisable fashion)
and was cruelly wounded. I learned about his time of
scrupulosity and severe penances when he lived in caves.
But I was most struck by his experience beside the River
Cardoner in Spain.

There the tormented spirit of Ignatius met a sweet and
temperate God of Love. Ignatius said he was taught many
mysteries in the way a schoolmaster would teach a child.
He was embraced and healed from much of his scrupulosity

and fear of judgment. It was only through the utter trust in God that began to flower at this time that Ignatius could give all to God: Take, Lord...my everything.

FOR REFLECTION AND JOURNALING

+ Can you write about a time that your image of God changed?
+ When have you felt most embraced by God?

CLOSING PRAYER

Consider...That you, my God and Lord, are working and somehow laboring within all your creatures for me,
You give all things being and preserve them as they are: able to exist, to live, to grow in you.
And you do the same for me. You willed to make me your temple, created in your image and likeness.
Come to this temple Lord, and inhabit the space you have made. Amen.
—based on the Spiritual Exercises of St. Ignatius of Loyola

Week Six: Day Seven

INTEGRATING THE MESSAGE

> ...the Holy One pervades our lives, breathes through us, explodes in us, aches in us, laughs in us, and permeates every fiber of our being with relentless and passionate love.
>
> —Barbara Fiand, *Prayer and the Quest for Healing*

I returned from the crisp, sunny high desert in Arizona to a Louisiana winter week of rain and bone-chilling forty-degree days. Right now, I feel the rain will never stop. I want to stay in bed and not get up at all. But I have this book to finish, and I must get up and write. I am sure you are hardly inspired by my sitting at the computer with gritted teeth. But I also know in full measure that you have many days such as this in your own life.

God is hidden in the stuff of our every days. I am blessed that I know that God is as fully present with me here, in this messy office with thirty-seven books scattered about like flopping fish and the ache that is appearing in my neck, as God was present in the high desert as psalm prayer resonated in my soul and I walked a beautiful desert labyrinth. The fires of God's passionate love are not quenched, even by the daily cold rainfall of a south Louisiana February.

FOR REFLECTION AND JOURNALING

+ Review your journaling for the week. What have you discovered as you examined your images of God? How are your plans for prayer proceeding? How does your prayer feel?
+ Are you feeling consolation from God, or do you have a desolate feeling?
+ Is God being expressed as joy within you, or is there an aching there? Do you feel God's love? Is this new, or an old feeling? Explain.

CLOSING PRAYER

God, reveal to us all facets of your healing love and your will for our lives. Breathe through us, just for today. Let us feel your life-force within us. Amen.

Week Seven

GROUNDED IN REALITY: WHO AM I, REALLY?

Having looked at our relationship with God,
And what may distort it,
We hold our loving God close
As we turn to our selves,
Strong and frail, wounded and blessed,
Filled with darkness and glorious light.
Who are we, really?
Do we see ourselves as we are?

Week Seven: Day One

IN THE IMAGE OF GOD

> Our life is a love story. Whether we are Christian or
> Jewish, or Hindu or Muslim, we believe there is a God
> who has called us into existence out of love.... [W]e are
> in an intimate relationship with our creator.
> —Max Oliva, *God of Many Loves*

> ...in the image of God he created them;
>   male and female he created them.
> —Genesis 1:27

I like to maintain an image of myself as optimistic, although there are many days I am not at all sure that is true! Because I value optimism, it was difficult for me to be around my husband's good friend. Let us call him Joseph. Joseph was almost relentlessly pessimistic about everything, especially about himself. A cursory look at his childhood revealed to me the reasons this was so, but I still argued with him all the time. (My husband was of much more use to Joseph's soul by simply accepting him as he was.)

One day when he was running himself down, I said, "Joseph, you shouldn't talk that way. Remember, God loves you."

Joseph paused for a long moment and then said sardonically, "Well, he must not be too particular." After I had smiled awhile at this comment, I wondered about it. Joseph thought that God saw as Joseph himself saw. Joseph could only see his flaws and imperfections, not the reflection of God's spirit within him.

Joseph is passed on now, and I believe he has discovered that place where he feels perfectly loved. I believe he now knows he was always created in God's image.

I have often read the words "God's image" from Genesis or heard them read aloud. What do they really mean? What would it mean to me if I accepted that I am created in God's image, that I am good, holy and strong? That I am creative, loving and life-giving? That my hands, if I so choose, are God's hands on this earth?

Have we forgotten that we are created in God's image because we have forgotten who we are? Do we think we are who other people tell us we are? If so, we have lost the sweet, insistent voice of God who says, "I created you out of my love to express my love on earth." We are the whole image and expression of that love. And God saw us, and knew that we were good.

FOR REFLECTION AND JOURNALING

+ How do you relate to these words, "We are made in the image of God"?
+ What does this knowledge mean in your life?
+ What keeps you from embracing this image of yourself, if anything?

CLOSING PRAYER

What can it mean, Spirit of Creation,
That I am made in the image of God?
I don't feel God-like.
I am filled with fears and small imaginings,
Petty angers, little resentments.
Not so thrilled with myself or my actions.
Am I an expression of your love?
Come to me, Sweet Lord,
And make it so.
Show me all the ways.
To be in Spirit with Spirit,
For Spirit alone.
Amen.

Week Seven: Day Two

OUR WOUNDS, OUR SELVES

> ...the LORD binds up the injuries of his people.
> —Isaiah 30:26

> Jacob was left alone; and a man wrestled with him
> until daybreak. When the man saw that he did not
> prevail against Jacob, he struck him on the hip socket;
> and Jacob's hip was put out of joint as he wrestled with
> him. The he said, "Let me go, for the day is breaking."
> But Jacob said, "I will not let you go, unless you bless
> me." So he said to him, "What is your name?" And he
> said, "Jacob." Then the man said, "You shall no longer
> be called Jacob, but Israel, for you have striven with
> God and with humans, and have prevailed."...
> So Jacob called the place Peniel, saying, "For I have
> seen God face to face, and yet my life is preserved."
> The sun rose upon him as he passed Penuel, limping
> because of his hip.
> —Genesis: 32:24–28, 30–31

Who are we really? This is the question that will resonate
through this week. We explored being made in God's image.
And yet we are wounded, broken in places, not able to live
as we would like.

A few years ago I directed an evening of reflection in my
home parish entitled, "Heal Me, Yahweh." A song of the same
name written by Vince Ambrosetti was sung by our choir and
movingly danced by my friend Sharon O'Neill. This deeply
emotional song speaks of our longing for Yahweh to heal our
wounds. It seeks a God who seems far away.

As I looked about the audience that night, I recognized
friends who had experienced loss in relationships, loss that

had affected their lives deeply. Connie's husband had died recently after a brief bout with cancer, a death that left her groping about in loneliness and shock. Another friend's wife had left to go to the far western United States in an attempt to make sense of her depression. Frequent calls and letters to her had revealed that she was moving further and further away from reconciliation with him. One church member, Sally, was reeling from the suicide of a daughter. The wounds went deep, and there was no hope but God, no way to make sense of loss without knowing that God cares and that the people of God care. As the tears flowed freely, love filled the room. It was a love that did not depend on circumstances, but on God alone. Many faced long spells of grieving, but a subtle ray of hope entered in, a turning toward the light.

The Bible makes a point to tell us that Jacob was wounded in his battle with God and that he bore those wounds for the rest of his life. Through his wounds Jacob had to wrestle with who *he* was. He had to be wounded in the ego battle before he could welcome God into his heart. He faced his battle courageously and asked for what he wanted. Despite his many faults he discovered that he was God's delight. He discovered this through the wounding experience itself. It changed who he was; his very name was changed.

FOR REFLECTION AND JOURNALING

+ As I read the story of Jacob I see that our wounds can bless us. It doesn't seem that way at the time. Our wounds are the very stuff of our wrestling with God. They break us and send us limping into the light. What wounds do you wish to journal about today? What questions do you have about yourself now?

CLOSING PRAYER

Choose your own prayer. Perhaps you would like to meditate on the wounds of Christ, or visit with Mary in her sorrow by saying a few sorrowful mysteries of the rosary or reading John 19:25–27. Perhaps you will ask God to begin to teach you how your wounds have made you who you are today.

Week Seven: Day Three

THE SELF FORMED BY SUFFERING

> If I recognized God—God the Creator, God the Spirit,
> the One who moves in and out of my life in disguise,
> would I finally arrive at the other side of this dream
> that insists that the meaning of my life rests in my
> circumstances?...The [Spirit says] at the heart of
> creation is My Delight, and it cannot be defeated.
> —Paula D'Arcy, *Seeking with All My Heart*

> If you view it as a journey into an ever-deepening
> encounter with God, this will keep it from becoming an
> abstract debate observed at a distance. We can't
> observe the question of suffering from a distance.
> Out of his greatest darkness comes Job's greatest
> statement of faith....It is purely a creation of grace, as
> faith always is.
> —Richard Rohr, *Job and the Mystery of Suffering*

As we explore the mystery of the parts of ourselves that are formed by suffering, I remember a time when I was much younger. I attended the funeral of a friend's mother, Martha, who had suffered much of her life with rheumatoid arthritis. I remember her hands, how crippled and deformed and painful they were. The homilist at her funeral service struck me with his words: "We know how much Martha suffered, and that her suffering is at an end now. However, we look at the Book of Job for encouragement." "Encouragement?" I remember thinking.

The homilist continued, "If the Book of Job does nothing else it shows us that suffering is not punishment. It is not a punishment for sin at all. It is the part of life that comes to us all. I know in Martha's life that it drew her to God and to truth." I couldn't really understand his words then. Unjust suffering just made me angry, not enlightened. And God himself seemed to injure us and cause us suffering.

But the world has turned around a lot of times since that day. My church has encouraged me not to try to explain everything, especially not right away, but to live with mystery. How rich our heritage of spirituality is in the Catholic church! How much it can challenge us to dig deeper and to walk in darkness without becoming bitter. I don't really understand suffering all that much more than I used to. But I understand that I just need to experience life prayerfully; it is not my job to explain everything and set it into neat categories. I am trying not to insist that the meaning of anyone's life rests in its circumstances.

And so today I can say with Job:

> For I know that my Redeemer lives,
>   and that at the last he will stand upon earth;
> and after my skin has been thus destroyed,
>   then in my flesh I shall see God,
> whom I shall see on my side
>   and my eyes shall behold, and not another. (19:25–27)

In the final analysis we need to know this: *God is on our side.* God is with us, suffering with us, crying with us. He sets us so close, so close to him, and takes our part. God cannot be defeated.

FOR REFLECTION AND JOURNALING

+ What is your reaction to the suffering of others?
+ What specific things come to your mind as you consider your own suffering and its impact on your life?
+ How do you cope with suffering in your life?
+ Does Paula D'Arcy's quote make sense in your own life? Explain why or why not.

CLOSING PRAYER

God speaks to us...
Set your affections on me, and keep them there.
Center your attention on me.
Yes, set your heart to follow me with singleness of mind.
You shall not be disappointed.
—Frances J. Roberts, *Come Away My Beloved*

Week Seven: Day Four

THE FALSE SELF FORMS IN SHAME

> I heard the sound of you in the garden, and I was afraid, because I was naked; and I hid myself.
> —Genesis 3:10

Continuing to look at who we really are, we begin to wonder: Why are we bound by negative emotions so much of the time? Why do we so fear what people think about us? Why do we so often feel that we are flawed more than others, just not up to standard? In these questions we come face to face with the reality of toxic shame.

The ancient story of the garden tells us that somehow, early on, toxic shame entered the world. The couple, walking in the garden, discovers that they are not equal to God and moreover they are naked before God, who sees everything. Having gone their own way, they don't realize they can go back in humility. They forget to say, "I'm sorry." Their now puffed-up egos lie and cover up, and they blame one another.

Psychologists and religious leaders (and our own common sense) teach us that some amount of shame and guilt make us human and are therefore necessary for our soul development, especially when these feelings move *through* us and cause us to repent when we hurt others. We have to keep our behavior in check as we live in a complex and peopled world. We desire to leave others uninjured by our actions.

True humility, then, means that we know our strengths *and* our weaknesses. We do not seek to be God, even though we know he has made us a little lower than the angels.

And yet, shame gone too far is not humility and can be one of the most debilitating of emotions; it changes our ground of being. We are Viola, singing happily in the choir, and something wounds us. We are deemed not good enough to sing life's song, and the message sticks.

We have gone beyond guilt here which says, "I did something wrong." We have entered into toxic shame that says, "*I* am a mistake. *I* am flawed and unworthy." These thoughts are held firmly below the conscious level. We then put on personas that hide who we are. We become performers and people-pleasers. Or we act tough and pretend that nothing bothers us. We can certainly lose track of what we *really* feel. We have become the false self and have lost all remembering that we are made authentically in God's image.

John Bradshaw, in his book *Family Secrets,* describes the effects of toxic shame in this way: "Toxic shame affects not just our doing, but our very being. Deep down we feel that something is very wrong with us. Toxic shame demands that I wear a mask, put on a disguise, develop a false self. If I were to let you see me as I really am, you would see that I am flawed and defective and reject me. I must therefore put on a mask and remain silent."[6]

The accumulated effects of toxic shame block God's voice. In our state of false self, we put on masks that refuse to let anyone know what we feel. Our defenses become so strong that not even the well-meaning and loving friend can come close to us. We try to be perfect or we are rebels and icebergs; we are not authentic. We are lonely, yet we dare not let you enter our loneliness. We will always tell you, "I'm fine."

Before the garden experience and *after,* God calls us into sweet, covenant love. This covenant, for the Hebrew people, symbolizes membership in a new family. We are heirs and relatives of God who seeks us and calls us good and makes us kinfolk. When we embrace this, while shining the light on our wounds, our shame can begin to heal; we can find our created selves again.

FOR REFLECTION AND JOURNALING

+ What is your felt reaction to this essay?
+ What is your felt reaction to the ideas of shame, guilt, masks and the false self?
+ What might be some characteristics of your false self?

CLOSING PRAYER

God, let me walk with you again in the garden,
In the cool of the evening. And you will tell me about
the ways I am made in your image, the ways that I am good.
You will sit with me and love me. And you will let me tell
you who I really am.
You will give me the acceptance that I cannot seem to give
myself.

How beautiful your garden is,
How kind your face and warm is your touch.
I look at everything you have made.
I look at myself, you made me too.
And everything you have made is good. Amen.

Week Seven: Day Five

BOWING TO A FALSE GOD

> If we are afraid to make a mistake because we have to
> maintain the pretense of perfection, because we still
> remember the bitter taste of parental disappointment,
> of a teacher's criticism or sarcasm, every time we did
> something wrong, we will never be brave enough to try
> anything new or anything challenging. We will only do
> things that are guaranteed to turn out right. We will
> never learn; we will never grow.
> —Harold S. Kushner, *How Good Do We Have to Be?*

> What place is there in me to which my God can come,
> what place that can receive the God who made heaven
> and earth?
> —Saint Augustine

> Confrontation of the shadow is essential for
> individuation, as Jesus made clear in many of the
> synoptic Gospels.
> —John Sanford, *Mystical Christianity*

As we explore our complexity and seek who we really are,
we encounter the ego within us. Our egos are not evil. They
are our executive function, the part that allows us to function in the world. But our egos only see a small part of reality. As we long for unity and seek after meaning in our

suffering and peaceful discernment, the ego is making other plans. It has plans for separateness and competition, for fear and discord. It strives mightily to change the outer circumstance and make us safe.

In the ego's world there is never enough to go around. We are urged by the ego to get what we want by besting another; in short, by being the best, by being perfect. This ego-driven worldview has largely taken over in our workplaces, schools and even neighborhoods. Competition and acquisition of new stuff is the rule. The ego is that part of us that will act to align us with our dominant culture. In this way the ego keeps us safe and unsanctioned by the culture we live in.

Dr. James Dobson addressed our acquisitiveness as he said recently on a radio program that we are selling all that is vital to us: our time, our relationships and our highest service to others in order to accumulate material goods that wind up discarded in the garage! And yet...we are driven to do so. When anxiety strikes, when emptiness calls, we might fill it with shopping or often we use other forms of getting ahead that will bring us society's praise. We don't try new things in the spiritual life; we continue to try to make our outer lives perfect.

We lost the place where God can come and be with us. We forget how to receive him. We forget who we are.

FOR REFLECTION AND JOURNALING

Let us look at some of the dominant values of our American culture. Do you agree with me that these are some of them? In what ways have these values affected your life?

+ Men are to be strong and in control, not showing their softer emotions.
+ Anger is forbidden in many families or an opposite is

reached where no one respects the other.

+ We strive to be attractive by every means at our disposal.
+ We value having things and looking good.
+ Work hard and be productive!
+ Cheer up!! (Stop thinking so much, get your head out of that book, do something useful.)
+ Competition is the order of the day.
+ We become uncomfortable talking about the inner life. Feelings are dismissed with platitudes: *That's just the way life is; oh, well, get over it; everybody feels like that; don't dwell on it.*
+ Consuming goods and services is a safe and approved thing to do.
+ Practicing real creativity is too risky. (We will be called odd, amateurs, wannabes, told we are having a midlife crisis, etc.)
+ We should always be aware of what people think! Be extra careful with everyone's opinion of you.

Our culturally held values may differ somewhat, depending on our location, age and other factors. Remember, I live in the Deep South. As I wrote the quote about anger, I thought about all the road rage we are seeing now and even the rudeness at stores and restaurants that is becoming prevalent. This is surely anger gone amok. Can we allow the shadow of anger to dance more freely when we are among strangers?

Other things may come to mind for you as dominant aspects of your culture. These are usually not gospel values. Living the gospel has nothing to do with looking good and having things. I know this, although I have failed at being true to gospel values as much as anyone else.

Not only are these not gospel values, but they are also a real danger that comes to Christ-self when the dominant, valued aspects of our society differ from those traits that God gave us and desires to grow in us. We so fear not fitting in; I know I do. We become masqueraders, or we no longer know who we are.

CLOSING PRAYER

We are saved in faith,
By the redemptive work of Jesus,
In our lives and in our world.
There is no better thing, no purer gold than this.
Let my life reflect the confidence,
That comes from knowing him,
Knowing Spirit and truth,
Knowing God and loving well.
Let my life be as free and beautiful
As the wildflower
that lifts its face
to the sun.
Amen.

Week Seven: Day Six

The time has come to confront the many masks in my life. My mask is not really me. It does not depict the trust self created in God's image. Perhaps getting in touch with the masks of my life can free me of unnecessary burdens. I don't really want to hide behind a mask.
—Macrina Wiederkehr, *Behold Your Life*

A friend of mine tells of attending a mask-making class years ago. She was instructed to place strips of gluey paper over her face, which had been smeared with petroleum jelly so that the mask could be removed. After the mask dried, she struggled to remove it and could not. She was about to panic when two women came to her assistance and wrestled the mask off her face. As she opened her eyes, she beheld the two dear women, loving her, without her mask.

We seek now to remove our own masks, the coping masks, the hiding-masks that have served us well. It's time to let them go. Hiding behind our masks we have become:

- The boy who is not athletic yet sits the bench day after day rather than pursue music, which he loves
- The woman who is not considered lovely and tries, with great pain, to refashion herself in the image of those who are deemed pretty (Consider our epidemic of eating disorders.)
- The gentle poetic man who hides all his feelings and becomes depressed
- The girl who dreams of being a writer yet forces herself to attend all the parties instead of staying home and writing in her journal as she wants to (Who wants to wind up alone with only cats for company?)
- The man who secretly values creating art above acquiring material things yet continues to work at a job he hates to buy a new boat
- The man whose unrecognized anger and sadness turns to high blood pressure, heart attack or stomach miseries
- The woman who feels devalued at work or at home yet does not allow herself to voice her feelings or seek change, finally having a breakdown
- The person who cannot speak inner truth to a religious or other authority
- The man who cannot tell his children that he loves them
- The man who longs for intimacy but can't express his feelings, his vulnerability

We learn to adapt to such a degree that the godly voice of authenticity becomes a distant whisper, no longer heard.

The true self is pushed down into the shadows. The false self is in control, along with its personas (perhaps our persona is the always hard-working, happy person) and false beliefs, such as: *If you really knew the real me, I would be rejected. You would be surprised and disgusted at the real me.*

We forget that we are the harbor for God who made heaven and earth. We forget that we are the "light of the world," and we hide furiously beneath our bushel baskets. Why do we shrivel in upon ourselves and refuse to live in freedom? Why do we surrender ourselves to ego demands? We ask God to break the chains of the false and too careful self and bring light to all our shadows. We long to live life— the life of the gospel—abundantly.

For Reflection and Journaling
+ What masks would you like to put aside today?
+ When you consider the work of Jesus, how did he help people put aside their masks and be real and authentic?
+ Do you know anyone who seems very authentic to you? Journal about this person and his or her gifts.

Closing Prayer
...You see me as I am for you are a God of no-masks. With firm and gentle hands remove the protective masks I wear. Mend the scared and scarred places in my life that I may put on the new self, created in your image. Amen.
—Macrina Wiederkehr, *Behold Your Life*

Week Seven: Day Seven
Beginning to Be Who We Truly Are

> 'Tis the gift to be simple, 'tis the gift to be free,
> 'Tis the gift to come down where we ought to be.
> —from a traditional Shaker song

The healing of the false self as we find our truth is an ongoing process. We don't do this by effort, but by awareness. We ask God to open our eyes and allow us to see ourselves realistically. I was reading some excerpts from the little book *Let Yourself Be Loved* today, and I encountered a woman who said, "I feel as though I am either on a pedestal or in the pit. I believe no one will love me unless I am perfect, but when I fail I feel utterly worthless."[7] The author tells us that as this woman began to explore, she found that the pedestal and the pit were both manifestations of the need to rigidly control her actions and so control others' reactions to her. When she failed to control another's reaction, she descended into darkness in the pit. She became more realistic about the fact that we are all a blend of weak and strong, good and bad traits. We don't heal by artificially trying to grow ourselves bigger and placing ourselves on pedestals. Nor do we become authentic by debasing ourselves and digging a pit for ourselves. We can't manufacture our self. It is there; we need to let it flow in through grace. We need to welcome it.

We heal with awareness of *all* that we are, and, to paraphrase Jesus, we are weeds and wheat growing in the same field. The woman started to realize that she didn't have to be a star to be loved. I must remind *myself* that I don't have to be star to accept myself.

In all vulnerability I can let you see who I am and trust that you will not reject me. This is a big step in healing. Let me tell you something surprising: When you let others see your flaws, they usually love you more! I have experienced this time and time again. Vulnerability leads to the intimacy that we so crave. Being vulnerable means letting yourself be loved.

FOR REFLECTION AND JOURNALING

Take some time now and look over your prayer journal for the week. You may want to highlight any strong themes or ideas that you see in your prayer. Do you accept yourself? What masks do you wear? What things do you do that you don't really want to do—and yet the culture around you expects these actions? What aspects of your true nature might be pushed into your shadow? What light is beginning to shine for you?

CLOSING PRAYER

God of love, keep me simple, yet, let me know
That I am the harbor for you.
May I be vulnerable,
May I invite intimacy in.
May I know you, the trustworthy.
Creative light, who made heaven and earth,
Make your home in me, God,
As I make mine in you. Amen.

Week Eight

GROUNDED IN WHOLENESS: JOHN 9

Having explored who we really might be,
in God's eyes and in our own,
we look at our blindness and our light.
We look at our broken parts, those we don't
acknowledge.
they are parts of us that need to be loved,
we welcome all parts of ourselves home so that we
may be whole.
Here is the good news: It is all right,
we are acceptable
just as we are.
All the parts of us,
put in their proper place,
can render service to God's will on this earth.
and further Christ's kingdom of love.

Week Eight: Day One

THE BLIND DISCIPLES: BEGINNING TO EMBRACE OUR SHADOWS

> As he walked along, he saw a man blind from birth.
> His disciples asked him, "Rabbi, who sinned, this man
> or his parents, that he was born blind?
> —John 9:1–2

Earlier in the week, one of my directees said to me wryly, pointing to her head, "Well, the committee has been in, and it hasn't been pretty." We can all relate to hearing those voices in our heads. They can certainly misdirect us. As Saint Paul said, we do what we would not, and don't do what we would. We are a puzzlement even, or especially, to ourselves.

In John 9 we meet a variety of people who, if we use a little imagination, can represent various aspects of our personalities. Some of these aspects are hidden from us; some we applaud and set on high pedestals in our personality. All can contain vitality when we welcome them home and integrate them into who we are.

Jesus seems to be locked in a virulent struggle with the religious leaders of his day. Just before this encounter with the man born blind, he has rescued the woman caught in adultery. He continues to tell these leaders who he is, and they give him the ultimate insult by calling him a Samaritan. They also say that he is possessed by evil forces. Now Jesus will summon his power again as he comes upon this unfortunate one, the man born blind.

First, let us take a look at the disciples' reaction to seeing this blind man. Their question seems to be totally of the head and not of the heart, "Rabbi, who sinned, this man or his parents, that he was born blind?"

We don't see compassion in their reaction, although it may have been there, hidden. In the disciples I see the part of me that distances me from pain by intellectualizing it. I don't see a person in front of me (the man born blind); I see a condition, a conundrum, a problem to which I can apply my mind. I see someone who doesn't fit in, an outcast. I need to figure out why he has come to this pass, so that I don't fall into the same trap.

I remember a time I acted this way during spiritual direction. Dear Father Condry, a cheerful soul well past eighty, was my spiritual director for a year. He was sunshine in my life. I often arrived at the retreat house for our meeting to find him whistling and sweeping.

One day I read him my journaling on the widow's mite. I brought what history I knew of first century Palestine, and described in detail what this sacrifice must have meant for the widow. Father Condry listened, and then he said, "But what does it mean to you?" I was surprised that I had missed that piece of understanding. I know that I am compassionate, yet I had distanced myself from my own feelings of vulnerability and giving away too much, my own sense of being depleted and used. At the same time, I knew I gave little of my material gifts to others. I pushed that sense of guilt into my shadow space.

Father Condry was patient with me, and Jesus is patient with the disciples. He answers that God's glory will be shown through this blind man—that he is not being punished for any sin by his disability. Here Jesus invites us to allow God's vision to invade us, to allow ourselves to see as God sees, even if it makes us uncomfortable. Following Jesus' example, we let ourselves feel and be present to each one whom we meet.

And so today, I show compassion for the part of myself that uses intellect to distance me from my feelings. I embrace the brokenness within me that doesn't want to feel, that wants to analyze rather than risk. This is a part of me that wants to know everything and be in control with that knowledge. I attempt the difficult balancing act of loving that intellectual part of myself while putting it in its proper place. I don't want my smartness and cool intellect to overwhelm the caring part of me.

FOR REFLECTION AND JOURNALING

+ Do you tend to intellectualize problems? Explain.
+ In what ways can you react to suffering, as the disciples did?
+ What is Jesus teaching us now?

CLOSING PRAYER

Heal my blindness, Lord, and help me to be whole.

Week Eight: Day Two

WHY AREN'T THE NEIGHBORS JOYFUL? OUR SHADOWS OF FEAR AND PESSIMISM

> His neighbors and the people who used to see him
> before (for he was a beggar) said, "Isn't this the man
> who used to sit and beg?" Some said, "Yes, it is the same
> one." Others said, "No, but he looks just like him."
> If God wants us to be grateful, it is not because God
> gets anything out of it. It is because thanksgiving
> means we are in touch with the reality of God's
> beneficence and will find joy in our gifts.
> —M. Basil Pennington, *Seeking His Mind*

The neighbors of the blind man have known him for many years. When they see that the man has been cured, they react curiously. They begin to argue about whether the man who now sees is the same man who had been born blind! Why aren't they excited for the man, now cured? Why do they deny what their own eyes are telling them? Is it fear that keeps them from believing and hoping that good things do happen? Are they so afraid of being duped in some way that they can't acknowledge with joy and gratitude the movement of God's great grace in their midst?

This is a small example, but once I was in a local office supply store, getting my latest ream of paper. Outside, a brilliant sun shone from a cloudless sky and the temperature hovered around seventy. As I checked out, I said to the lady behind the register, "What a beautiful day. Wow!" She lifted her head toward the glass storefront with a quick glance and said, "Well, that will soon change."

Poor lady. Now maybe she was bummed out because she was stuck behind a register while other people came and went in freedom during that beautiful day. But I imagine her remarks had more to do with attitude than situation. Some of us just can't latch onto the good. Perhaps we have been disappointed too often. Perhaps we feel that life has not given us the good things others have, and yet we can all enjoy a beautiful day!

The blind man's neighbors represent those parts of me that push the good away. Those parts that are too pessimistic, feel too unworthy, hide out too well, or have become too hardened to life's gifts. Those parts that say, "If you never get excited about things, you will never be disappointed."

Perhaps, too, this is the part of me that feels that another's good fortune diminishes me. I feel too cut off from the community to rejoice with another. This is a light-starved part of me. I seek to love and heal those parts of myself today.

FOR REFLECTION AND JOURNALING

+ In what ways do you react to good news as the neighbors did?

+ In general, are you optimistic or pessimistic? Explain. Why do you think this is so?

CLOSING PRAYER

Heal my blindness, Lord, and help me to be whole.

Week Eight: Day Three

OUR SHADOW PHARISEE

> Some of the Pharisees said, "This man is not from God, for he does not observe the sabbath." But others said, "How can a man who is a sinner perform such signs?" And they were divided. So they said again to the blind man, "What do you say about him? It was your eyes he opened." He said, "He is a prophet."
>
> The Jews did not believe that he had been blind and had received his sight until they called the parents of the man who had received his sight....
> —John 9:16–18

> It takes compassion to own a part of yourself that you previously disowned, ignored, hated, denied, or judged in others. It takes compassion to accept being human, and having every aspect of humanity within you, good and bad. Ultimately when you open your heart to yourself, you will find you have compassion for everything and everybody.
> —Debbie Ford, *The Dark Side of the Light Chasers*

The Pharisees certainly are not excited about this healing miracle, either. They were concerned about what the rules were and *who had power.* In fact, their clinging to power hardened their hearts to love and joy. Their slavish devotion to rules wrung all the loving kindness from their hearts. They were concerned about Sabbath healings, and who did the healing, and they, too, denied what their eyes showed them. Knowing the man well, they said, "It must be another man." I am sure they had stepped over him in his helplessness during many days when they gathered in the temple square. He didn't even seem like a person to them, merely an object.

And so, I come face to face with the Pharisee within me. I don't know about you, but I am beginning to know my Pharisee well. This is the superior part, the part that does things right and demands that everyone else *follow the rules!* It is the part of me that puts looking good above goodness.

I was appalled to see this part of myself dance out from the shadows when there were recent changes in the Liturgy of the Eucharist. The funny part about this whole thing is that I had fussed about these, "Silly, nitpicky, little changes," such as bowing during part of the Creed, bowing before receiving communion, and standing at a different time during the prayer. "Doesn't Rome have more important things to worry about?" I fumed.

Then, when the changes took place, I was chagrined to see myself watching others to see if they bowed at the right time! If I had to do it, so did they. Yuck! I didn't like the way the new rules brought out the Pharisee in me. This is a minor example, and I soon caught myself. But there are other times when my Pharisee nature is hidden from myself. I hurt others with my arrogance, my blind adherence to *what we are supposed to do, and what we have always done.* I hang onto power in groups or gatherings, seeking attention and my own way. I even take the highest chair. This blocks intimacy in my life. Others can't come close because I am playing ego games and not being authentic. Grabbing for power at the expense of others is not holy, and it is certainly not a lovable trait—and I do desire the love of others.

The interesting thing is that the Pharisees are driven by fear. Fear hovers around much of our shadow personality. The Pharisees fear loss of power; they may fear for their own salvation (this healing does not fit in their system); they fear change. Theirs is not the God of love, but of rules. The certainty-seeking and power-seeking part of me that lives in fear is the Pharisee within. I also fear looking bad and losing my place in the "in" group. I seek to love that part of me that lives in fear of loss, that part that seeks certainty through my own performance.

FOR REFLECTION AND JOURNALING

+ What parts of you can seem pharisaical at times?
+ Do you sometimes become cold and distant, or tied to the rules? Harsh? Explain.

CLOSING PRAYER

Heal my blindness, Lord, and help me to be whole.

Week Eight: Day Four

THE PARENTS ARE AFRAID: SHADOWS OF FEAR WITHIN US

"Is this your son, who you say was born blind? How then does he now see?" His parents answered, "We know that this is our son and that he was born blind; but we do not know how it is that now he sees, nor do we know who opened his eyes. Ask him; he is of age. He

will speak for himself." His parents said this because
they were afraid of the Jews....
—John 9:19–22

Sit with your friends, don't go back to sleep.
Don't sink like a fish to the bottom of the sea.
...
Life's waters flow from darkness.
Search the darkness, don't run from it.
...
Be a wakeful candle in a golden dish.
—Jelaluddin Rumi, *Love Is a Stranger*

This story gets curiouser and curiouser as we encounter the
parents of the man born blind. Try to imagine yourself in
their place. Your child has just been healed of a permanent,
life-altering disability. He was blind, now he can see! It's a
miracle! They should be jumping for joy, they should be
grateful to Jesus, but they are governed by fear also.

This is the part of me that is resistant to change because
other people might not like it. Instead of embracing my own
truth (now I see differently) I shrink away in fear that others might not approve. I am afraid to claim the workings of
God within my heart because powerful people in my life, or
even a part of myself, might not approve. I hang onto outmoded ways of doing things, and I replay old tapes in my
head merely because it feels comfortable to do so. *This is
what I have always believed. How can I leave my beliefs now?*
I am afraid to search the darkness; I run from it.

Recently, I had a prayer partner named Max who after
years and years of overworking and experiencing too much
stress had a breakdown. We painfully tried to put the pieces
of his life back together in a new pattern. He tried to see the
good that had come out of worlds of pain.

When Max had the breakdown he was forced to reorder his life and turn over to others responsibilities that he had carried. One day Max said, "Well, this breakdown had to happen because my company wouldn't have *let* me slow down otherwise."

His words jangled dissonantly within me. A man who for years had heard his body, mind and spirit crying out to him for relief (or did he not hear?), yet he can't slow down because his company wouldn't *let* him. If they had said no to his changes, would he have sunk like a fish to the bottom of the sea?

I didn't confront Max with his own words. Perhaps I should have. But I see with God's help that he is rapidly reclaiming his inner authority. He can celebrate the workings of grace, redeeming that part of him that is becoming like the light of a candle in a golden dish.

Sometimes he feels that I am the only person who understands his inner growth and need to change, but God does, too. It is enough. Max goes on with a heart filling with hope and gratitude.

I invite the parent figures within me to come forward and replay their old tapes. I must face both their truth and their falseness within me. I must see my fears and my whining for what they are: a part of me. And I must embrace with love these parts of me that live in fear and can't move toward new things.

These are examples of old tapes and truths, that we may be called to leave behind:

+ If I work hard to please everyone, I will be appreciated.
+ *My* church doesn't make major mistakes.
+ America, love it or leave it.
+ It is always better to give than to receive.

+ Don't rock the boat, keep your nose clean, and you will come out a winner.
+ God loves best and rewards greatly those of us who do everything "right."
+ Better to be safe than sorry.
+ This was good enough for my parents, and it is good enough for me.
+ Be nice to others and they will be nice to you. (Always.)
+ People deserve what they get.

Many of these taped messages operate below our conscious level. In fact, just saying them out loud makes some of them sound foolish, but we often proceed as though they were completely true. The grain of truth in these old messages can keep us hanging on to them. Yet, as we let these old tapes go, we tune in to the authentic parts of ourselves, the parts that want to tell us all of the truth and bring all of our heart into consciousness.

The parents of the man born blind direct all questions to their now-cured son. And here we encounter the fully redeemed part of our personality.

FOR REFLECTION AND JOURNALING
+ Do you relate to the parents of the blind man in any way? Explain.
+ What rigid, outmoded or fearful ideas do you sometimes encounter within yourself?
+ Do these attitudes keep you stuck? Explain.

CLOSING PRAYER
O, heal the darkness of my mind,
And bring all my thoughts to light.
Let me grow to full maturity and flourish in your sight.
Amen.

Week Eight: Day Five

CLAIMING THE HEALING OF OUR BLINDNESS: INNER AUTHORITY

Becoming conscious—"living in the light," is hard work.
—John Sanford, *Mystical Christianity*

Courage serves as the foundation for personal empowerment. Empowerment means taking control of your life....It is the refusal to allow other people to tell you who you are.
—Robert J. Furey, *Called by Name*

So for the second time they called the man who had been blind, and they said to him, "Give glory to God! We know that this man is a sinner." He answered, "I do not know whether he is a sinner. One thing I do know, that though I was blind, now I see." They said to him, "What did he do to you? How did he open your eyes?" He answered them, "I have told you already, and you would not listen. Why do you want to hear it again? Do you also want to become his disciples?"
—John 9:24–27

He healed the darkness of my mind,
The day he gave my sight to me.
It was not sin that made me blind;
It was no sinner made me see.
Let others call my faith a lie,
Or try to stir up doubt in me.
Look at me now, none can deny,
I once was blind and now I see.
Ask me not how!
But I know who has opened up new worlds to me.
This Jesus does what none can do.
I once was blind and now I see!
—Fred Pratt Green, "He Healed the Darkness of My Mind"

The only person who seems to be without fear and able to speak the truth is the healed man. Despite pressures, he speaks the truth as he has experienced it. I had an experience on retreat recently that shook my own inner authority.

There he sat before me, my worst nightmare: Someone who did not like me, and didn't approve of my work.

I was directing my very first men's retreat at Our Lady of the Oaks in Grand Coteau. The men had never had a woman director, and I was rather green in working with an entire group of men. I had a partner, Bob, who shared speaking and counseling duties with me. This helped. I thought the whole retreat was going really well.

Then this man, let us call him Josh, came in to my office appearing friendly and open. He spoke of himself and his family. But then, using the same relaxed tone, he began to criticize me and my partner severely.

"I was excited when I started this retreat, because you guys are educated, but this is the most poorly organized thing I have ever been to. I don't know what this retreat is about. Your talks don't have any substance. You talk down to us, and we are better than that."

In a single moment, my inner authority shriveled and retreated to a tiny corner of my being. I got the outline of the retreat and explained to Josh shakily what material the retreat included and how we were following the Spiritual Exercises. I asked him if he had done any of the many journaling and prayer exercises we had supplied. He nodded in a dismissive way.

The retreat changed for me that day; fortunately, it was toward the end of the weekend. I began to question every word that exited my mouth. I was angry, hurt and sad. The child within me was scared. The woman within me heard all the old tapes of male superiority that I had worked mightily to ignore. It would have been easy to brand Josh as a Pharisee and let it go at that. I could have projected all my angst upon him, that wretch! (All right, I did that some.) But how would this make me grow and get any better at the work I did?

And why did I expect myself to be perfect and to please everyone?

I fretted and worried. If I am honest, I must admit that I *did* want everyone to love me. Because of this, I was being a perfectionist and placing the emphasis of the retreat in the wrong place. In my worry, I decided that Josh represented a tip of the iceberg and that many of the men didn't like my speaking. I later received my evaluations and there was only one (guess who?) negative evaluation among forty participants. (Funny that Josh is the one I write about today! Rats!)

Through this experience and others, I am realizing that releasing my perfectionism would be a relief. (I am working on it.) I learned a lesson about doubting my goodness when confronted with criticism. I needed to practice releasing panic and to encourage the wiser and more secure parts of myself to take over when needed. All in all, I needed the inner authority of the man born blind.

This once-blind man now cured is filled with this inner authority. He knows that God has healed him, and he fully embraces it. He will not deny the wonder of gift that has come into his life. He can stand against persecution because God has built a home in his heart and come to dwell. It is not all about *him*. It is about the wonder-workings of Grace.

This man is totally transformed, yet he speaks carefully only of the truth *he* knows. He says only, "I was blind, but now I see." He also knows that the judging and fearful parts (of this story and of our own hearts) will try to deny the gifts, and are not the friends of the true self. He will converse with the neighbors, the parents, the Pharisees. He even asks the Pharisees (somewhat sarcastically) if they are interested in following this Christ of love. His anger against them is justified. They have certainly never tried to help him.

His questions make the Pharisees furious, as they would have to release their power and their knowing in order to entertain this unknowing. They send this miracle man away. They are blind to love, yet they think they see.

The man born blind stands alone, as we sometimes do. Yet he is not just healed, he is remade. Empowered. He has come into his own life, his true self. He no longer allows others to tell him who he is!

I did work on my talks (after Josh) and tried harder to be clear about what I desired to communicate. But I also accepted that I will never please everyone. (As I write this, I realize that I am just *working* on accepting this. It is not a completed task.) This is hard for me, and yet it gets easier the more I practice finding the good inner authority within. I guess eventually I will be grateful to Josh. Just give me a little more time...

FOR REFLECTION AND JOURNALING
+ In what ways do you feel like the cured, once-blind man?
+ How do you think you would have reacted to Josh?
+ Is your inner authority strong? Becoming stronger? Why do you think so, or not?
+ What is calling out within you to be transformed?

CLOSING PRAYER
Choose a part of John 9 that speaks to you. Write this in your journal and use it as your prayer. Recall these words during the days to come.

Week Eight: Day Six

JESUS, WE PRAISE YOU: TEACH US TO BE LIKE YOU

> Never since the world began has it been heard that
> anyone opened the eyes of a person born blind.
> —John 9:32

One evening at retreat after I had spoken on the subject of the healing of the man born blind, an ophthalmologist came into my office to give some special background on this story. He explained that when children are born blind because of problems with the outer eye, that if those problems can be corrected early in life, the neural pathways for sight can develop normally. However, if these problems are not corrected in childhood, these pathways don't develop, and in fact wither away. Even for physicians with all their modern craft, healing blindness becomes almost impossible at this point.

The fact that Jesus cured a man *born* blind was astonishing. It was astonishing because Jesus did not just cause cataracts to fall away from the man's eyes, or do a similar work on the outer eye (as amazing as that would be to us). No, Jesus actually caused all the withered nerve pathways to the brain to be healed and opened. The doctor told me that evening that, because he knew this about blindness, that he had developed a special respect for Jesus' healing powers when he studied this Scripture.

Developing trust in Jesus' healing powers is a part of this prayer journey. We give to Jesus those parts of ourselves that need to be opened up, enlightened. Our withered hearts, our weary souls, our falseness and our sin.

In addition, Jesus becomes for us the model of someone living through the true self, the self connected to God.

Because of this deep and abiding relationship with his Abba, Jesus was strong, brave and resilient. He placed compassion toward the hurting as his highest value. He was able to act authentically despite the disapproval of all around him. Because of his connection with the source of all life, his inner divinity blazed forth in a unique way, never seen before or since. Jesus, we praise you.

FOR REFLECTION

+ What qualities do you see within Jesus that you would most like to emulate?
+ How are these qualities beginning to show forth in you?

CLOSING PRAYER

You will discover that the more love you can take in and hold on to, the less fearful you will become. You will speak more simply, more directly, and more freely about what is important to you, without fear of other people's reactions...trusting that you communicate your true self even when you do not speak much.

The disciples of Jesus...had come to live a deep connectedness with him and drew from that connectedness the strength to speak out with simplicity and directness, unafraid of being misunderstood or rejected.
—Henri Nouwen, *The Inner Voice of Love*

Jesus, let me hold on to your love and release my fear.
May I stay connected to you always. Amen.

Week Eight: Day Seven

CONSTANTLY BEING RECREATED

We are still looking for signs—the dramatic healings, the apparitions, the whirling sun and so on. The real

> sign, the miracle, is not in these eternal happenings,
> but in the inner conversion of mind and heart.
> —Gerard W. Hughes, *Seven Weeks for the Soul*

> He said, "Lord, I believe." And he worshipped him.
> —John 9:38

Each day, a new beginning. A day to have wounds healed. A day to believe. A day to welcome home parts of ourselves that we have refused to embrace. These words about beginnings, written in books here and there, are a special comfort to me when I lose my temper, talk too much and hurt people's feelings, act compulsively, or succumb to deep, deep laziness of mind, body and spirit.

I am thinking about this now in a very mild way because I just got back from Wal-Mart where in the checkout line my hand took on a life of its on, darted out and snagged a pecan praline. I glanced at the fat grams on the back of the package; I think it said 14, but I squinted and kind of pretended it said 1.4. The praline surely did taste good; I ate it slowly, and I was grateful for it. So much for the low-fat pasta I had for lunch!

Well, tomorrow is another day. Isn't that the wonderful thing: that we begin anew each day? We are constantly being created and recreated within. God is dedicated to our inner conversion, the illumination of our sight. We are given the ability to believe. This gives me burgeoning hope, not about avoiding pralines, but about developing my courage and gratitude, my inner authority and my compassion. We turn again to the truth that we are created in God's image and unconditionally loved. This is the bedrock of all our healing and restoration. God loves us with our extra pounds, our sagging cheeks and the faults that keep haunting us. Father Richard Rohr says that we can do two basic things about our faults: we can recognize that we have them, and we can try not to hurt others with them. They probably will never completely go away; they are a part of our personalities. And yet, God loves us and enters into our hearts to create us anew again and again.

FOR REFLECTION AND JOURNALING

+ In what ways do you start afresh each day?
+ Did you enjoy journeying through John 9? If so, in what ways?
+ As you read over your journaling for the week, discover which parts of yourself you are welcoming home. What strong themes or questions do you have?
+ Do you see what is authentic within you?
+ Do you have any confusion? Fear or relief? Anger? Trust? Journal about these things.

CLOSING PRAYER

O, heal the darkness of my mind and heart.
Let me see my heart just as you do.
Don't let me try to split myself apart,
But bring me now to wholeness within you. Amen.

Week Nine

SURROUNDING OURSELVES WITH HEALING

We began to heal our inner sight,
And bring our scattered selves home.
And we desire to be healed and converted in other ways, too.
Growing in wholeness now, we praise
Jesus, the same, yesterday, today and tomorrow,
Come, Jesus,
Come and heal.
We will be whole in you.
For service in your kingdom.

Week Nine: Day One

TOUCHING THE HEM OF HIS GARMENT

> Jesus brought a message of freedom: from slavery to
> the letter of the law, from physical illness for some,
> from possession for others, from sin as in the case of
> the paralytic, from humiliation and shame as, for
> example, for the woman accused of adultery (John
> 8:1–11), and from fear as when he walked into the
> locked upper room after his resurrection.
> —Max Oliva, *God of Many Loves*

> When poets talk about the human soul, they do not
> talk about reason, they talk about feeling. The totally
> human human being, they enable us to see, is the one
> who weeps over evil, revels in goodness, loves
> outrageously, and carries the pain of the world in
> human hands.
> —Joan Chittister, *Heart of Flesh*

> As I prayed, I saw Jesus before me, healing the people.
> I was transfixed and drawn by his presence. I fell to my
> knees before him. He touched my hair and looked into
> my eyes. He asked, "What is it you want?" I said,
> "Please, Lord, heal me and make me whole."
> —from the personal prayer experience of another

As a woman, I identify deeply with the hemorrhagic woman
from Luke's Gospel. Being a woman can be very difficult at
times, as we cope with our biology year after year. But for
this woman, biology had gone berserk. Her constant bleeding had ruined her life. She was desperate and dying by the
time she encountered Jesus.

She was also filled with deep and wounding shame. A
glance back at the customs of her time and place tells us why.
Women were considered ritually unclean when they were

145

menstruating. They were isolated and could not handle certain things, touch their husbands or sons, and so on. This was manageable for a week during the month, but this dear lady had become *unclean all the time* in the eyes of her community. She was damaged goods, deemed not worthy of normal life. She could not marry (or if already married, her husband would have little to do with her); she could not work or have a social or religious life in her town or village. She was as shunned as a leper. In addition, she was probably severely anemic, lacking energy and life force, and she had spent everything she had on treatments that had not helped her. She must have felt truly rejected by God as well as man.

In the act of touching Jesus she violated the social codes of her day. This is why she recoiled in fear when Jesus realized what had happened. It is interesting to note that Jesus didn't actively *do* anything here. It was her faith that drew the power from Jesus, the power that healed her.

Ron Rolheiser, the author of *The Holy Longing,* likens the community of believers to the hem of Jesus' cloak. We are healed within a community of faith, especially if we are now in a healing group that meets on a regular basis or if our church community or friends can hold us close. We are healed within our churches as we struggle together to stop the bleeding within our lives. The hem of Jesus' cloak clothes us with love and gives us courage. The Liturgy of the Eucharist feeds us together, and the words we hear read aloud begin to sink deeply within us. There comes a day when they mean something personal, something real. The words heal us then.

This woman has been healed by the power of the cloak at her weakest and most emotional hour. I have noted in my life and in the lives of those I walk with in spirituality that it often is in our passion that God touches us—or, like this woman, we touch God. In our deeply feeling state we become like Jesus, we weep over evil, we carry the pain of the world, and sometimes it is the world of our own hearts. In extremis, when nothing has helped and nothing is working, we call out to God. Our faith draws us to him; we feel his touch, we are surrounded by the gospel garment.

This woman was certainly passionate in her desire to be delivered and had exhausted every human means to be healed. She took a risk. She reached out. Her faith healed her because she acted out of vulnerability, not ego.

But not only was her body healed; she also was healed from shame, from the falseness of unworthiness. Jesus looked at her with compassion. He did not care about the law; he praised her. I want to be like Jesus. I want to place people above rules and social strata. When I do, perhaps Jesus will say to me, "Your faith has made you well."

FOR REFLECTION AND JOURNALING

+ What groups in our society suffer the stigma of shame?
+ What aspects of himself does Jesus reveal in this healing story?
+ Have you been healed in a dramatic way? Explain.
+ Explain how you do or do not relate to this woman.
+ In what ways is your community helping you to heal?
+ Who in your life, besides yourself, needs healing? Can you help?
+ Try to do the examination daily. It will be a help to your spiritual practice.

CLOSING PRAYER

I touched you,
and you said to me, "Your faith has healed you."
I touched you, and you looked at me with love.
Just the fringe of your cloak, the edge of your garment sustains me.

Your burning love fills the air about you
and fills my heart.
Amen.

Week Nine: Day Two

A PARALYZED SPIRIT

> We grow in love when we grow in gratefulness. And we
> grow in gratefulness when we grow in love.
> —Brother David Steindl-Rast, *Gratefulness, the Heart
> of Prayer*

> When Jesus saw him lying there and knew that he had
> been there a long time, he said to him, "Do you want to
> be made well?"
> —John 5:6

As we continue looking at the healing miracles of Jesus, this is an interesting one. Even odd. Some of the parts don't seem to fit together. Why did this man lay there for so many years?

People in similar need often help one another. I have seen this many times at hospitals, when the families of the chronically ill run errands or sit for one another, bring messages, or just talk about their shared problems. Sometimes lifelong friendships are forged around sickbeds.

This spirit of community does not seem to be present at the healing pool near the Sheep's Gate, where one man waited for thirty years to be put into the water at just the right moment. I must admit that I am skeptical. I wonder if the group at the pool was really that callous. I wonder if the paralysis that the man was enduring did not extend to his spirit as well. There may have been something within him that held back from being healed, from accepting the responsibility that wellness would bring.

At any rate, when Jesus asks him what he wants, he begins to whine a bit, and he tells Jesus why he has not been able to be healed. The man is counting on the magical powers of the pool to end his suffering; he doesn't seem to understand the part he must take in his own healing. Then, suddenly, he encounters the Compassionate One who says, "Stand up, take your mat and walk." Gone is any physical weakness that the man may have had; he now has the strength to pick up his sleeping mat and walk. He leaves his unconscious, paralyzed life behind and follows Jesus into the Temple. Then Jesus says, "So do not sin any more, so that nothing worse happens to you."

Now, why did Jesus say this? He makes it clear throughout the Gospels that sin is not necessarily—in fact, not usually—the cause of illness. However, this harkens back to my earlier point. This man's spirit was paralyzed. How this has come about, we are not told, but perhaps we can relate to it. I know there have been times when I felt paralyzed, unable to move forward or backward. It occurs to me that perhaps this man was depressed or so shame-filled that he couldn't claim healing as his own. He did not have enough life force within him to seize hold of a normal, productive life.

Jesus, then, desires to heal the man of his shame as well as his paralysis. He wants to heal the man's false and powerless self. He warns him not to return to the old ways, not to stay in a dance of death with his old, shame-filled past. And yet, the man doesn't seem very grateful. He seems more resentful that the old games won't work any more. Perhaps he had become too comfortable with his very passive way of life.

We can be initially resentful when we are called to healing. We become defensive: "What's so wrong with me anyway? I'm doing all right." This attitude in the heart of this frozen man is almost humorous, yet we can be the same as our shame begins to heal. There is that within us that resists. Certain things can happen to plunge us into the fires of shame again; our weakness becomes our sole reality. John Bradshaw names this *the shame spiral.* And it spirals down! We become our smallness and lose sight of the God within. I had a severe shame spiral when I encountered Josh on the retreat. His words gave voice to my worst fears about myself and awakened all my own negative, destructive voices.

If we have enough unmitigated shame spirals we will turn (again, perhaps) to drinking, controlling or fixing others rather than ourselves, to drugs, overwork, overbuying or whatever our addiction may be. Or we just retreat into old patterns which, while not life-giving, are comfortable and safe.

God wants more for us than lives controlled by shame. An antidote to shame is gratitude. I can stop and see all the goodness in my life. I can rejoice with the richness of *what is,* and I can know that God loves me in the particular, in my very shape, in the *now.* I acknowledge now that the God who brought me this far will not abandon me.

Granted, there are many times that I don't feel like being grateful, yet as Henri Nouwen says, "Still it is possible not to belong to those (negative) powers, not to build our dwelling place among them, but to choose the house of love as our home."[8]

FOR REFLECTION AND JOURNALING

+ In what ways do you relate to the author, or to the experience of the paralyzed man?
+ Do you feel stuck in certain areas of your life? Explain.

+ What small steps could you make that would bring you more life?

CLOSING PRAYER

List four things in your life that you are thankful for.
Say a prayer of thanksgiving for these things.

Week Nine: Day Three

NAMELESS, FAMOUS EARLY EVANGELIST

> Because we are so afraid of nonsuccess, of being a refugee, not having a home, afraid of the opposite masculine or feminine parts of our own souls, we marginalize whoever represents those parts of our soul that we deny.
>
> —Richard Rohr, *Job and the Mystery of Suffering*

> ...he left Judea and started back to Galilee. But he had to go through Samaria. So he came to a Samaritan city called Sychar, near the plot of ground that Jacob had given to his son Joseph.
>
> A Samaritan woman came to draw water, Jesus said to her, "Give me a drink." ...The Samaritan woman said to him, "How is it that you, a Jew, ask a drink of me, a woman of Samaria?"
>
> —John 4:3–5, 7, 9

Once in speaking to a group I asked them, "If Jesus were alive today, where would he be? What group would he spend time with and minister to?"

I suggested that perhaps Jesus would be in our poorest neighborhoods where drugs, guns, prostitution and abuse run rampant. He would be walking with his arms around gay people, perceived criminals and those with AIDS. He would be comforting those whose presence in our midst we find most difficult. The marginalized.

And I also prayed that Jesus would be with people like me, too, the middle class, the overfed, the comfort-driven, the status-haunted, for we too are poor in spirit. We, too, need Jesus. I know *I* do.

In the beloved story of the Samaritan woman at the well, we encounter a person filled with shame and outcast by society. She was the target of gossip and snide remarks. We don't know why she had so many husbands, but we do know that a woman had great difficulty surviving in those days without a man to support her, be it father or brother or spouse. The state of marriage was hardly a choice; it was a tool for survival. Yet she had obviously failed, and things had gone terribly wrong. The last man who claimed her as his dependent didn't even marry her.

As we have often heard, as a Samaritan she was looked down on by the Jewish orthodox community, and because she was a woman no self-respecting Jewish man would chat with her beside a well. Samaritan. Woman. Sinner. They loved their dividing labels then, just as we do now. When we use these labels we can project all the things we don't like about ourselves onto another, they can embody our shadow for us. This wounds them and makes our wholeness suffer. We act out of falseness and turn away from loving ourselves and others.

Jesus came into this shadowy, divided world and turned it on its head. In this mystical meeting, he ignored division and poured sweet water into the heart of the rejected one.

FOR REFLECTION AND JOURNALING

+ What people are marginalized in our society? How could you reach out to them?

+ In what ways do you feel like this woman?

+ What aspects of himself does Jesus reveal in this passage?
+ What graces do you ask of Jesus for yourself today?

CLOSING PRAYER
God, you are a God of grace
Who bends to touch me in every hurting place.
I need you, Spirit, Creator, Friend, Brother, Sister, Mother God,
Living Word!
Be with me all the day.
Send living water to refresh me until I sit in quiet with you again. Amen.

Week Nine: Day Four

SHE DRINKS DEEPLY OF LIVING WATER...

> We cannot measure how you heal,
> Or answer every sufferer's prayer.
> Yet we believe your grace responds
> Where faith and doubt unite to care.
> The pain that will not go away.
> The guilt that clings from things long past.
> The fear of what the future holds.
> Are present as if meant to last.
> But present too, is love which tends the hurt,
> (love) we never hoped to find.
> To mend the body, mind and soul,
> And make your broken people whole.
> —John Bell, "We Cannot Measure How You Heal"

This unlikely woman, this outcast Samaritan, (I wish we knew her name) became one of the first evangelists for Jesus. How could this happen? How did guilt and fear become transformed by love into love alone? Once again, we see all that is known and accepted turned upside down and inside out.

This woman, stricken in body, mind and spirit, came to the well in the heat of the day. This was not accepted practice. Most of the local women came to the well in early morning when it was cool, and the water could then be used for all the chores of the day. They congregated there, as we do at our health clubs, school drop-offs, water coolers and checkout counters, and they spoke of what was on their minds. Ah, yes, they even gossiped.

This woman didn't want to encounter this "in" group. She was outcast—even from the outcast Samaritans! She was the scarlet woman, the trashy one. She had been with too many men, and she was scorned. So she went at the hot noon hour, heart heavy, barely hanging on, to get water from the well.

Author Joyce Rupp says of this state of being, "Most of the time we search without really being aware of what it is gnawing at us deep inside. We search for something called happiness. We long for a gift named peace. We search for meaning in our lives, for love, for understanding of ourselves and others, for an acceptance of the ups and downs of the human condition."[9]

The woman suddenly finds all that she has been searching for with a parched and hungry heart. She encounters a life-changing force and learns about the healing waters, those waters of eternal life. She is told that the waters of Spirit can well up *within her.* That she can worship God in spirit and in truth. She is included by Christ in his healing, gathering work. She has become a part of the kingdom.

Like the healed man who was born blind, she fully owns her truth. She is no longer afraid of those who have scorned her. She cannot measure how God heals and yet she shares her healing and she shares the Lord with everyone! She is a new person; she knows she is loved and accepted. The Hebrew word for salvation connotes *being made well.* This echoes the old spiritual: "All is well; all is well, with my soul."

FOR REFLECTION AND JOURNALING

Ignatian Prayer Experience: Take some time, in your imagination to visualize the scene beside the well on the dusty day that Jesus met the Samaritan woman. You may want to enter as a bystander or as the woman, or as a disciple or even as Jesus himself. Try to hear, see and smell what is around you. If you like, you can engage one of the characters in conversation. After you meditate on this, write about your experience.

CLOSING PRAYER

Pray the initial hymn that began this story. Take it into your heart.

Week Nine: Day Five

JESUS HEALS THOSE WHO HAVE TRIED TO GO IT ALONE...

> He entered Jericho and was passing through it. A man was there named Zacchaeus; he was a chief tax collector and was rich. He was trying to see who Jesus was, but on account of the crowd he could not, because he was short in stature. So he ran ahead and climbed a sycamore tree to see him, because he was going to pass that way. When Jesus came to the place, he looked up and said to him, "Zacchaeus, hurry and come down; for I must stay at your house today." So he hurried down and was happy to welcome him.
>
> —Luke 19:1–6

I recently submitted some program ideas to a prayer group to which I belong. The group didn't like the ideas and told me politely that other things were planned. Although I agreed with a smile on my face, when I got home from the meeting, I felt stung, rejected and alone. I lay on my bed and prayed about these feelings. I knew intellectually that the women were not rejecting *me,* yet in some part of me, I felt stinging rejection. My old demon, sensitivity, rose up with renewed strength. It made me play with ideas of just leaving this group. (Well, I'm just taking my ideas and going home!) This would be an unjustified action that I would regret. The child within me became the cold six-year-old on the playground with no playmates. I had to spend some prayer time holding and comforting my child and speaking to my sensitivity and my low self-esteem. I had to ask God again to heal these parts of me. I am a strong and accomplished woman, I thought, with lots of weak and hurting places.

I am like Zacchaeus, up in the tree. Here is a rich man looking on from afar, feeling rejected. He had thought that the way to feeling good about himself was to attain money and power. This he did, but he is still needy. His smallness represents his low self-esteem. Now here he is up in the tree, looking for what is real. Looking for healing and forgiveness and belonging.

As I read this passage, I note that Jesus doesn't wait for Zacchaeus to repent of his old ways before he announces that he will visit. He just sees the need and the longing within this man. He sees the hurting places. With his ever-present compassion, he reaches out to bring this Zacchaeus into his fold. He will heal this strong and accomplished man with lots of weak and hurting places.

FOR REFLECTION AND JOURNALING

+ In what ways do you feel like Zacchaeus?
+ Has low self-esteem been an issue in your life? Explain.
+ Do you sometimes react out of sensitivity or abandonment issues?
+ In what way do you long to be more connected, more involved or accepted by others? Is intimacy an issue for you? Can you let yourself be vulnerable before others?
+ What aspects of Jesus' nature are evident in this story?

CLOSING PRAYER

What is this you say to me, Jesus?
I'm up in this tree, I can hardly hear you.
You want to sup with me today?
You want to enter my house?
Sorry, it's not clean enough, I'm not good enough today, things are messy.
I had an argument yesterday; it wasn't pretty. I'm still sad about it.
I dozed off in church on Sunday, I admit it, I was bored.
I forgot to mail my check to that charity I said I would support.
So you see, I need you to come another day, when I have gotten my act together.
What? Today's the day? You say you will help me clean things up?
You say it all...doesn't matter?
Well, all right, come it. Tell me more about this.
The way I'm doing it all now doesn't seem to be working so well.
And by the way, Lord.
Thank you.

Week Nine: Day Six

PERSEVERE IN PRAYER

> Devote yourselves to prayer, keeping alert in it with
> thanksgiving. At the same time pray for us as well that
> God will open to us a door for the word, that we may
> declare the mystery of Christ....
> —Colossians 4:2–3

In the evenings when we are about to go to sleep and before
we put him in his sleeping kennel, our English bulldog
Beau loves to get on our bed and make me scratch him. As
long as I keep one hand on him, even if I scratch him only
a little, he is content, and I can read my book or watch TV
and not even really look at him. But if I take my hand off of
him, he almost immediately bats at me with his big paw to
remind me to put it back! He will do this over and over. Dee
and I laugh at him and his persistence.

We, too, need persistence. Sometimes our healing journey seems long. But in our persistent prayer we ask God to
keep his hand upon us and bring us home to him and to ourselves. In persistent trust, we know that God will do this.

FOR REFLECTION AND JOURNALING

+ Are you persistent in prayer? Why or why not?
+ What is unfolding in your journey today?
+ What circumstances in your life are foremost in your
  mind? How is healing entering your life, if it is?
+ What old wounds are still there, exerting their influence?
+ Are you growing in love for self and others? In accept-
  ance? Be honest with the page and with yourself.

CLOSING PRAYER

Lord, may I persist in prayer,
Coming daily to your temple.

You wait for me here, always.
You never tire of me,
Why should I ever grow weary of seeking your face?
Forgive me, God, when I become lazy or disinterested,
Too caught up in the world to visit with you,
talk to you and seek your will, your loving will in my life.
Amen.

Week Nine: Day Seven
STAYING IN THE LOVE OF GOD

> You do not need to make plans nor resort to any clever strategy. Keep yourself in the love of God. Pray in the Spirit. Rejoice evermore. Set your affections upon Christ.
> —Frances J. Roberts, *Come Away My Beloved*

We have looked this week at Jesus as he actively healed and converted those he walked with so many years ago. We believe that he desires in the same way to heal and to be with us. I hope you have embraced in a new and deeper way this image of Jesus as healer. His was a heart filled with compassion for the suffering he saw around him. His was a heart that reached out to the little ones and still reaches out to all that is little within us. I hope that in your life you will visit the healing miracles of the Bible often and embrace them for yourself.

FOR REFLECTION AND JOURNALING
+ Look back over your prayer journal for the week and highlight peak experiences.
+ In what ways do you long for healing?
+ Which gospel healing was the most powerful for you?

+ Are there other gospel healing miracles that come to your mind? Journal about them.
+ In what ways do you long for inspiration? Write in a personal way about these issues.

CLOSING PRAYER
Close with a Hail Mary or other prayer of choice.

Week Ten

SURROUNDING OURSELVES WITH FORGIVENESS

We are discovering healing and conversion of heart,
In many forms and ways,
And now we embrace
Forgiveness
As the heart of the spiritual journey.
One might almost think that we are on this earth to learn
to forgive
ourselves and others.
And yet, it is a misunderstood subject.
We can't force our hearts to forgive.
What then is the answer?

Week Ten: Day One

HOW CAN I FORGIVE?

> But not all the moments you have shared with friends
> and family have come close to the sacred. You have
> swallowed your bitterness when charity turned to
> hostility. You've seen a friendship end in cold anger. You
> and the other person were never able to bring the
> problem out into the open. After a while, your insides
> turned to ice. You have been surprised by betrayal and
> abuse.
> —Eddie Ensley and Robert Herrmann, *Writing to be
> Whole*

> It is true, of course, that forgiveness does not happen at
> will and needs prayer and grace. Forgiving too readily,
> because, after all, that is what one is supposed to do,
> can backfire, and one can find oneself years later
> transferring the anger one has not worked through or
> the hurt one has not dealt with onto somebody else.
> —Barbara Fiand, *Prayer and the Quest for Healing*

Yesterday was truly a miserable January day. It was bone-chilling cold and raining. The dying Christmas tree hung around, useless, in my living room, depressing me. My directee Laura, upon entering my home with coat, scarf and umbrella said, "This is our worst weather. Faulkner wrote about this kind of day." I agreed. I had been trying to get warm all day, and the cold grayness seemed to be reflected in my soul as well.

We couldn't meet on my little porch (too cold, too many windows) so I ushered Laura into my bedroom space, all tidied up for her arrival. I had lit candles and arranged a dark green rocking chair and another chair over the patterned area rug. Laura settled in with her usual array of books, and we centered ourselves in prayer. My mood became more peaceful.

Laura had been struggling for several months with her relationship with her mother and her other siblings. She felt that these relationships represented lifelong struggles for healing in her life. Therapists she had seen had told her that her family was characterized by codependency. Laura had not spoken to her mother in several months after a plan to place the older woman in an assisted living facility had "blown up in everyone's face." But, Laura said, this was just the culmination of so many years of struggle with her mother's emotional illness. Her brother came to the rescue from another state and backed his mother up. Mom was to stay in her home, regardless of the strain on others. Another sister—the sister that Laura felt was caught most deeply in the web of her mother's manipulations—was caring for her mother daily.

Laura was troubled by gospel messages to forgive or one would not be forgiven. These passages brought out her anger. How was she to forgive a lifetime of pain? Was this what God was really expecting...you know, keep turning the other cheek again and again? We talked about what it might mean to forgive, what did the word mean, after all? It was a word used by so many, layered over with all sorts of meanings: the refusal to take revenge, letting go, not feeding anger, releasing. These terms seemed as confusing to Laura as the original word.

Laura surprised me on this gloomy day by showing me a book by Dennis, Matthew and Sheila Fabricant Linn. I am a big fan of their work, and often have bought multiple copies of their books to share with those I directed. I had not seen this particular book, *Don't Forgive Too Soon: Extending the Two Hands That Heal.* In this book the authors develop a wonderful idea for forgiveness. They liken it to the grief process and advise their readers that often, depending on the severity of the hurt, the wounded one must go through all the grief stages. These stages are:

+ Denial
+ Anger
+ Bargaining
+ Depression
+ Acceptance

The stages were identified by psychologists and utilized by Elisabeth Kübler-Ross in her groundbreaking book *On Death and Dying*. They can be very useful to us as we struggle with healing the wounds within our lives. In the days to come, we will explore these stages of forgiveness.

FOR REFLECTION AND JOURNALING
+ What are the major forgiveness issues in your life?
+ Would considering these stages of grief help in your forgiveness? Explain.

CLOSING PRAYER
God, grant me the serenity
To accept the things I cannot change,
The courage to change the things I can,
And the wisdom to know the difference.
Amen.

Week Ten: Day Two

DENIAL AND FROZEN EMOTION

A split between divinity and humanity has taken place in you. With your divinely endowed center you know God's will, God's way, God's love. But your humanity is cut off from that. Your many human needs for affection, attention, and consolation are living apart from your divine sacred space. Your call is to let these two parts of yourself come together again.

—Henri Nouwen, *The Inner Voice of Love*

The first stage we encounter in our forgiveness journey is denial. Denial is a natural defense mechanism that protects us from feeling all the pain of a hurt at one time. Denial serves a purpose, but if carried on too long, it can have harmful effects.

I saw an example of this when recently I directed a retreat at St. Charles College in Grand Coteau. There I met Frank, who was about sixty-five. I perceived Frank as somewhat cold and angry (his anger was at an unconscious level), and he exhibited a lot of resistance to the activities of the retreat. He sometimes challenged me aloud and, in general, I found him difficult. Later I was surprised to discover that Frank had signed up to see me individually. When he came into the office, he sat and folded his arms. Then he said, "All this feeling stuff, feel, feel, feel. What if you don't feel? What if you don't feel anything?"

Then Frank told me that he had been divorced for eight years. He had not wanted the divorce; his wife had left him for another man. He told me that life had pretty much been "the pits" since then. He had no social life and little interest in anything outside his home. He had planned to spend his retirement years traveling with his wife, but now he had no plans of any sort.

Frank assured me that he did not feel angry about what had happened. "What good would that do?" he asked.

I could see Frank's anger but he himself did not experience it as such. He had worked hard, without knowing it, to remain in the stage of denial. He didn't want to feel the deep feelings that his divorce had brought forth in him, and, in fact, was now aware of little feeling within himself at all. I didn't blame him. Who wants to hurt, to feel pain? And yet...it seems that we cannot pole vault from deep hurt to an accepting forgiveness. It just doesn't work that way. Denial isolates us and prevents others from helping us through our trials. We have to let our needs become known to us before they can be healed.

I tried to convince Frank to obtain counseling or spiritual direction on an ongoing basis. I knew that it would take time for him to break through his denial and begin to unthaw his emotions. I, too, feel denial when things I don't like happen. It is as though the whole world slows, and I get very stoic. My heart backs up within me and my head gets busy solving the problem, even if to solve it is not realistic. I am often surprised when the emotions of the event blindside me weeks or months later. Denial begins to give way to sadness, and sadness to anger.

FOR REFLECTION AND JOURNALING
+ Do you recall times when your emotions felt frozen?
+ Have you experienced the denial stage of grief and forgiveness?
+ How do you relate to Frank's story?

CLOSING PRAYER
Lord, thaw the recesses of my heart,
And let the love flow again. Amen.

Week Ten: Day Three
ANGER!

> Save me, O God,
> for the waters have come up to my neck.
> I sink in deep mire

where there is no foothold;
I have come into deep waters,
    and the flood sweeps over me.
—Psalm 69:1–2

In the wilderness our fear gives way to sadness and our sadness to anger. We need our anger, for it helps us to find our way.
—Mariann Burke, *Advent and Psychic Birth*

As I write these words this morning, I remember the time three years ago when I was betrayed in a cruel, laughing way by someone I had perceived as a friend. I remember trying to work through the betrayal. I had feelings of being lost in the wilderness without a map.

I got stuck in the anger stage of grief and unforgiveness for many months. I could find no foothold. I felt like a moth trapped in the cage of my anger. It generalized and I felt angry at everything and everyone. This was a dark and miserable place to be. I would think I was getting over it, and then some event would trigger a new onslaught. I alternated between feeding the anger and pushing it away. The event of the betrayal brought up many feelings of unworthiness in me. I felt like the emperor with no clothes; I had been found out. I wasn't worthy of love and respect; I made people too angry. The fact that many other aspects of my life and my relationships refuted this stance seemed lost to me. My thinking was not rational.

The Linns suggest that we befriend our anger and see what it can teach us; that we just be with it, without either condemning it or feeding it. Anger is a normal emotion and often signals to us that we have been violated. Anger should not be pushed away as sinful. It is the most misunderstood emotion, and our pushing it away can leave us devoid of life and clueless about the needs of our inner lives.

When we are angry, we may want to use physical exercise (this I did—I remember beating up the water of the swimming pool) and speak of our anger to those who will love and support us without urging us to either get over it quickly or take revenge.

In fact, in the case of anger and many of our other emotions, we must find *the third way,* that way that negotiates between violence to others and disrespect for ourselves and our own needs. This way asks that we think creatively about what response (not reaction) we can make.

In looking back to the time of my betrayal (and it still affects my stomach, but just a little), I can see that I would have been much helped by (after some time had passed) speaking to the one who hurt me. I talked myself out of this many times because it was embarrassing, and I convinced myself that this person wasn't worth it, had a heart of stone, and didn't care. (Maybe I was also embarrassed to show my anger to him, and my vulnerability.) Even though there may be some truth here, I ignored how this conversation might have dissipated my own anger. In general, however, confronting one who has hurt us, especially a family member, may not be a good thing to do. The healing must occur within us. Yet, I had downplayed my own strength in saying that I couldn't handle it. I missed the opportunity to tell this person, calmly, what his actions had cost me emotionally.

FOR REFLECTION AND JOURNALING

+ In general, how do you handle anger?
+ Are you angry at anyone, including yourself and desiring to heal this anger? Explain.
+ Could these methods of sitting with and healing anger be helpful to you?

CLOSING PRAYER

At a day of recollection recently, Father Whitney Miller said this about prayer: Do we say what we mean and mean what we say? He said we should note our intentions closely when we pray prayers that we have memorized and prayed many times. Do we mean, or at least *want* to mean what we say? Thinking about this statement, pray the Lord's Prayer.

Week Ten: Day Four

ATTEMPTING TO STRIKE THE BARGAIN

> I am weary with my crying;
>> my throat is parched.
> My eyes grow dim
>> with waiting for my God.
> —Psalm 69:3

During our bargaining stages, Kübler-Ross tells us we begin to maneuver and seek to be rewarded for good behavior. We manipulate. We bargain with God and others.

When I was hurting, I asked that *other people* act in a certain way so that *I* could get over my pain. This is also the time when we revert easily to a Santa Claus notion of God. Bargains made with God are the stuff of legend and TV shows: "God, if you just get me out of this, I will never, ever miss Mass again! Or I will never get angry over small things. I will give money to the poor." We resolve to be so good that nothing like this will ever happen to us again.

We see forms of this bargaining present in those dealing with loved ones who have addictions or illnesses. There is nothing that can't be given, no stone left unturned if only *this condition will cease to be.* If we are in codependent relationships, our own health, wealth, peace of mind and spirituality can be sacrificed for the sake of someone who will not or cannot change. We are left depleted and exhausted.

On the other hand, we may resolve to forgive if others apologize and admit we were right all along. We will forgive if they get their just punishment, highlighting how good *we* always are. Since these scenarios rarely happen, we are stuck with our bargaining; it doesn't work. We also can become very frustrated with God when God doesn't seem to move as we hoped. He continues to let the rain fall on the just and unjust. We say with the psalmist: "How long shall the wicked exult?"

However, if we pay attention to our bargaining, we can gain insight into possible creative solutions to our problems. We have to try to relax and be patient with ourselves in this stage.

FOR REFLECTION AND JOURNALING

+ Have you bargained with God? Journal about this.
+ Have you attempted to get others to conform to your wishes? In what areas and what ways?
+ Are you making progress in the area of forgiveness, or is this not a major issue for you? Explain.

CLOSING PRAYER

God, grant me the serenity
To accept the things I cannot change,
The courage to change the things I can,
And the wisdom to know the difference.
Amen.

Week Ten: Day Five

THE FORGIVENESS JOURNEY

> Freedom is possible through a mysterious,
> incarnational synthesis of human intention and divine

grace. The issue is not simply whether one follows personal attachments or follows God. It is instead a question of aligning one's intention with the God within and with us, through love and in grace....Jesus proclaimed a message of radical forgiveness, not only forgiveness of humanity by God, but also forgiveness of one another by people....Nothing...has to remain as an obstacle.

—Gerald G. May, *Addiction and Grace*

When Laura read my draft of her experience with her mother, she reiterated. "Lyn," she said, "remember it wasn't just an incident that brought me to this place. It has been a lifetime of trying to cope with my mother and all the family dynamics. Looking back, I think perhaps she has always had some serious mental health challenges. But of course, a child doesn't know that." And because the layers of pain had developed over time, it made perfect sense to view the forgiveness path as a *process* that would take place over time.

In working with the Linns' book, Laura saw that only a *process* of forgiveness could peel back the many layers of hurt that had settled in her heart over the years. I agreed; in fact, I wished I had had the book *Don't Forgive Too Soon* when I was first working on forgiveness issues in my own life. I identified with the authors in that I often moved to pacify or soothe the one who hurt me instead of taking time and assessing the needs of all involved, including myself. The emotions that lead me to forgive too soon are unworthiness, shame and fear. This type of pacifying leads to the original wound being suppressed and the anger not going away. (Again, this depends on the severity of the wounding.)

Laura was encouraged by the process and said she felt that in many ways she was between the bargaining and acceptance stages. One thing to consider is that we don't necessarily float through these stages neatly and in order. We can go forward into some acceptance and then go back into anger or depression for a while. We need to be patient.

Laura was seriously considering phoning her sister for lunch, although she wasn't ready to see her mother or her brother yet.

You may have serious forgiveness issues in your own life. And, as Laura and I agreed, often the hardest person to forgive is ourselves. Our negative emotions cause us to ask, "What kind of person am I that these things happen to me? Why do I react like this? Why do I mess things up so much?" These can be helpful questions, but our questions need to center more on our behavior and less on our basic shame and perceived flaws as human beings. Again, we forgive ourselves just for being human, belonging neither on a pedestal or down in the pit.

FOR REFLECTION AND JOURNALING
+ Continue to reflect on forgiveness of self and others. What obstacles to freedom would you like to remove?

CLOSING PRAYER
God, grant me the serenity
To accept the things I cannot change,
The courage to change the things I can,
And the wisdom to know the difference.
Amen.

Week Ten: Day Six

RESTING IN GOD'S LOVE
Practice the Abba Prayer, introduced on page 102–103.

Practicing forgiveness is hard work. We can certainly overdo working on ourselves and our inner lives. We need to seek balance. Today you may be busy with someone else's needs. You may enjoy a sport or work in the garden. Exercise and healthy food keep us in balance. We also need to get plenty of rest, as much as we can during any healing process. Recent studies have shown that sleep that comes before midnight is the most healing; so try to get to bed early whenever you can. Try to observe areas where you overdo things and relax about them, too.

God desires that we rest in him. God desires that we find peace in him. God desires that we find joy in him.

FOR REFLECTION AND JOURNALING

+ Where do you overdo things?
+ When do you sleep best?
+ Do you make taking care of yourself a priority?
+ Journal as you wish. You may want to draw or paint, move to music or walk outdoors. Pray as you wish. But don't skip this day. It is important to you.

CLOSING PRAYER

I see now, my Companion God,
How my life is a landscape of anger and love,
Of tornados and volcanoes,
Of quiet streams and welcomed retreats.
Walk with me over this landscape now,
And visit with me the places
Where my earth cries out for healing
And forgiveness.
Let us together with gentle hands
Fill in the spaces and heal the breaks
Within the paths of my life.
Amen.

Week Ten: Day Seven

THE SWEET LAND OF FORGIVENESS

> Each of these stages [of forgiveness] is like a chapter in
> a story, revealing a part of ourselves that we are
> tempted to push away. The human psyche is such that
> when we deny any part of ourselves we are no longer at
> home within, and we lose our connectedness as well.
> —Dennis, Sheila and Matthew Linn, *Don't Forgive Too
> Soon*

Jesus always told us that we needed to forgive in order to
be forgiven. I think he was encouraging us to see the
wounds within ourselves as well as the wounds of others. If
we can embrace our on imperfections with love, then we can
begin to understand the failings of those who hurt us. We
can see the reasons for limitation in their lives. As we practice compassion, we become more connected with all people
and all life.

Today, consider whether you are forgiving toward yourself, or if you continue to beat yourself up over past errors or
perceived errors. Do you continue to push parts of yourself
away? We have all made mistakes, some serious and some
not so. We have stumbled into serious sin. We have reacted
in anger, hurting others, often those closest to us. We have
been insensitive to the needs of people around us. We have
succumbed to laziness when we should have pressed on to
the goal, and we have pressed on toward goals that we
should never have taken up. Such is the stuff of life. And so
we seek now to forgive ourselves as we forgive others.

FOR REFLECTION AND JOURNALING

+ Look over your prayer journal for the week, and consider
  carefully those areas of your life's landscape that are call-

ing for the healing that forgiveness brings. Are you learning to be compassionate toward yourself? Are there significant others that you are beginning to forgive more?
Explain.

CLOSING PRAYER
Forgiving God, your fingers are gentle
As they touch the hurting places within me.
They heal my need to be right, my need for revenge.
The warmth of your touch
Softens my pride.
Knowing I am loved fully,
Let me forgive myself and others, my God
as you forgive.
Then I can say, Amen, Lord,
Amen to all you are doing in my life.

Week Eleven

IMMERSED IN THE PASCHAL MYSTERY

As we learn to forgive,
To grieve and move on,
We find the paschal mystery deepening in our lives.
As you did, Sweet Lord,
we die and rise,
we suffer and are resurrected.
Let it all be gift for your kingdom, our Brother,
Bread for your table.

Week Eleven: Day One

WHAT CAN DEPRESSION TEACH US?

It is for your sake that I have borne reproach,
  that shame has covered my face.
I have become a stranger to my kindred,
  an alien to my mother's children.
...
When I made sackcloth my clothing,
  I became a byword to them.
—Psalm 69:7–8, 11

Present day society is afraid of depression.
—Judith Duerk, *Circle of Stones*

The truest sympathy is found in those who, with the
strength of love, come out of the sunshine into the
gloom and dimness of others, to touch wounds tenderly,
as though their own nerves throbbed with pain.
—Fulton Sheen, *Guide to Contentment*

If he is allowed to express his sorrow he will find a
final acceptance much easier, and he will be grateful to
those who can sit with him during this stage of
depression without constantly telling him not to be sad.
—Elisabeth Kübler-Ross, *On Death and Dying*

Take my yoke upon you, and learn from me; for I am
gentle and humble in heart, and you will find rest for
your souls. For my yoke is easy, and my burden is light.
—Matthew 11:29–30

I know when I am flirting with depression because I become
uncharacteristically nervous and flighty. I make unnecessary trips to town and buy things I don't need. My mind
races, much more than usual. My usual messiness at home
escalates, and I can't settle enough to clean up. Yet I want
to be in stores where everything is new and clean and

bright, offering me the promise of a life that is neat and shiny. I am running from myself. If my depression deepens, the world turns gray. I am sloughing through my days. I forget what I used to like to do. Lacking energy and motivation, I feel hopeless and mired down in life.

In the depression stage of grief or forgiveness, we find that our bargaining didn't work. Others (even God) refused to do what we wanted; we are thrown back upon ourselves. Depression may be triggered by an event such as losing a job or facing an empty nest. It may turn up as we begin to look at long pushed down feelings. Regardless, our resistance to *what is* makes us miserable.

Depression may come as unhealed memories surface or when we try to forgive. We are facing loss. If we are ill or hurting we may become grim and refuse to communicate. We face our own powerlessness. Nothing we have done has worked to change the situation. God may seem far away and unconcerned. We feel sad and all the things we used to enjoy pale and no longer attract us. We may not sleep or eat well, and we may experience muscle pain, stomachaches or other ailments. If you begin to feel hopeless or deeply depressed, don't hesitate to consult a physician. God uses all means to heal us.

FOR REFLECTION AND JOURNALING

+ Have you or others close to you experienced depression? Explain.
+ What helps you when you are depressed?

CLOSING PRAYER

Have mercy on me, Lord Jesus Christ,
For indeed, I am a sinner
Who has been sinned against.
Amen.

Week Eleven: Day Two

CONTINUING THE STRUGGLE WITH DEPRESSION

> You have to move gradually from crying outward—
> crying out for people who you think can fulfill your
> needs—to crying inward to the place where you can let
> yourself be held and carried by God, who has become
> incarnate in the humanity of those who love you in
> community. No one person can fulfill all your needs.
> But the community can truly hold you. The community
> can let you experience the fact that, beyond your
> anguish, there are human hands that can hold you and
> show you God's faithful love.
> —Henri Nouwen, *The Inner Voice of Love*

> During an (inner) drought emotions are dried up. Like
> water, they may exist somewhere underneath, but we
> have no access to them. A drought is a tearless time of
> grief. We are between dreams. Too listless to know our
> losses...
> —Julia Cameron, *The Artist's Way*

> By the rivers of Babylon—
>   there we sat down and there we wept...
>
> ...
>
> How could we sing the LORD's song,
>   in a foreign land?
> —Psalm 137:1, 4

Yesterday I sat with a group for peer supervision in spiritual direction. We discussed the possible differences
between depression and a dark night of the soul. In the
prayer journey, times of desolation are described as dark
nights, when the comfort and nearness of God disappears

179

and we are filled with darkness. However, the individual in the dark night often holds on to the meaning of his or her journey, and holds on to hope. The person is still able to function at work and in the family at a fairly high level. Eating and sleeping patterns are not severely altered.

In clinical depression, an individual may not eat or sleep well, or may eat and sleep entirely too much. The person may not be able to go to work, or his job performance may fall off drastically. Hope seems gone. There are thoughts of suicide, perhaps.

These two categories are often not so neat and tidy, and it takes discernment to decide which group you may fit into when you have darkness in your soul. It is a good time to seek counsel and a listening ear. You may decide to visit a physician for an evaluation for clinical depression. Milder forms of depression may be grief working through the psyche and will ease with time and care.

The depression stage of grieving or forgiving often develops because we have now turned our anger in upon ourselves. We are refugees in a foreign land.

We begin to play tapes over and over about what we *should* have done: "I never do anything right!" "I shouldn't have stayed in that job so long." "I should have tried to write professionally long before this; I'm old now!" "I have such a hard time making good friends." "I am a terrible Christian." "Why did I say that to her?" And so on. And so on.

Our guilt, shame and anger threaten to overwhelm us. We may become "inner victims," not seeing a way out of our suffering. We feel like our depression won't end and things won't get better. In the worst-case scenario, we lose our hope for a better tomorrow. We are truly caught between dreams.

If you are depressed and in a group, ask them to hold you in love as they listen. Or you may be called to do this for others.

Sometimes we have to heal the severity of our depression itself before we can heal other things in our lives. I have gleaned suggestions from Kübler-Ross, Bradshaw, the Linns and others. I hope these suggestions help you or another.

Continue to pray even though it is difficult. Ask God directly to heal your depression. Honor your depression by attending to your inner life. Accept yourself.

Pray in whatever way nourishes you.

Attend church and be with your community, even though you may want to completely withdraw.

As a Christian, try to believe that your suffering has meaning and will lead to growth.

Remember that depression may have lessons to teach and that it will dissipate when the lessons are learned. Gently ask yourself what the depression might be teaching you. Journal about this.

Seek a spiritual director or companion.

Defend yourself to your inner, critical voices. Saying things such as, "No, I often do many things well," or, "No, I still have time to write," or, "Many people do love me," may help you gain control over this unhealthy chattering.

Try to get some physical exercise every day. You won't feel like doing this. But a simple walk around the block may be a healing start.

Know that many depressions will simply end with time. Hold on to hope, and get help if needed.

Talk to helpful, balanced friends who will find a middle way between encouraging your victim status and dismissing you. This is not easy and may not go perfectly. But, as Henri Nouwen says in the opening quote, we seek to let others hold us.

Often it helps to speak to a professional such as a personable, caring priest, spiritual director or therapist. Be honest with them about how you are feeling.

Tune in to your senses: cuddle your pet, listen to music, take a bubble bath, and cook a colorful, nourishing meal. Put flowers on the table.

Read about how others have worked with their depression. Most bookstores have large self-help sections.

If depression continues too long, affects quality of life severely, or threatens to overwhelm you, get medical help. You may have a chemical imbalance, and/or you may need therapy to help you regain your balance.

FOR REFLECTION AND JOURNALING

+ Have you encountered depression as you sought to forgive someone? Explain.
+ Have you experienced dark nights in your prayer journey?
+ Do you think that any of these strategies would help you to move out of depression?
+ Is there a depressed person in your life who you need to reach out to?

CLOSING PRAYER

Be with me, Lord,
when I am in trouble,
be with me, Lord, I pray.
Amen.
—Marty Haugen, "Be With Me"

Week Eleven: Day Three

SWEET SURRENDER

> Father, if you are willing, remove this cup from me; yet,
> not my will but yours be done.
> —Luke 22:42

I shared retreat work with a lovely lady named Sarah. She spoke to our group one evening, using as her Scripture Jesus' agony in the garden. I was surprised to hear that it was one of her favorite Scriptures. She explained to me and the group why this was so.

When Sarah was a much younger woman, raising four children, her life looked dark. She and her husband had hired a financial manager who invested their money and paid their bills. The manager was dishonest and stole at least some of their funds. He neglected to pay their house note for several months, and they faced losing their home.

When Sarah got the foreclosure papers, the season was Lent, which seemed appropriate. She had been in agony for many days, and she plotted revenge strategies in her head against the financial consultant. She was filled with anger and hate. On this particular day, she put her children down for a nap and began to pray the sorrowful mysteries of the rosary. She was engulfed with sadness as she prayed over Jesus' agony in the garden just before his crucifixion.

Sarah began to weep uncontrollably as she fully entered into what Christ has suffered. She knew that he had to fight within his own heart before he fully surrendered. Now, as she wept, she felt her heart softening. She began to accept her situation and put herself and her family under the wings of God's care. *Your will, Lord...your will.*

Sarah fell asleep and slept for three hours. She says that by some miraculous chance, her children slept that long also, which they never did. When she awoke, she was filled with peace. She and her husband worked through their problems. I can't remember now what happened with their house. I guess that wasn't the part of the story that Sarah emphasized. But I know that their lives regained peace and purpose and balance. Healing and forgiveness occurred. It is the same in our own lives as we work through the stages of our grief or unforgiveness and then surrender to God's time, God's care. Healing comes on gentle feet, and we are surprised by peace and joy.

FOR REFLECTION AND JOURNALING

+ What are you called to surrender? Your plans, your own way? Your pride or hostility?
+ What areas or events in your life have you surrendered to God's care?
+ Are there exterior areas of struggle that you may need to surrender?
+ Parents, look closely at your relationships with your children. Is surrender being called for?
+ Will surrender be a part of forgiveness for you? Explain.

CLOSING PRAYER

God, grant me the serenity
To accept the things I cannot change,
The courage to change the things I can,
And the wisdom to know the difference.
Amen.

Week Eleven: Day Four

PRAYING THE PASCHAL MYSTERY

Read prayerfully Luke 22.

Through the trials in the garden and beyond, our spirituality is called into maturity. We are called to see a God actively present within our suffering. God is not removed and unchanging toward us; he is the God revealed in Jesus whose very being was moved by the suffering of those about him.

And when Jesus himself was called to suffer, he suffered deeply, even calling out, "My God, my God, why have you forsaken me?" And yet, in the end he endured his suffering with courage, dignity and love, and lived again!

In smaller ways, perhaps, but with the same qualities, we seek to endure our suffering with dignity when we cannot change the conditions that cause it. We ask for the strength to move through it. We ask for eyes to see a God who is present with us supporting us with all God's being.

Now we see that God is...

The one who:

Grieves with us.

Cradles us.

Rocks us.

Touches the hurting places.

Soothes us.

Inspires us.

Listens to us.

Counsels us.

Holds us.

Accepts us.

Cries with us.

Helps us.

Calls us into the kingdom.

Brings new life.

Leads us into the service of Love alone.

FOR REFLECTION AND JOURNALING

+ What reflections do you have about suffering in your own life or those near you?

+ What reactions did you have to the Scripture passage?
+ Do you allow yourself time and space to be loved by God, especially when you are suffering? Explain.

CLOSING PRAYER

And so I understand that any man or woman who voluntarily chooses God in his lifetime for love, he may be sure that he is endlessly loved with an endless love which makes that grace in him. For he wants us to pay true heed to this, that we are as certain in our hope to have the bliss of heaven whilst we are here as we shall be certain of it while we are there.
—Julian of Norwich, *Showings*

Week Eleven: Day Five

ACCEPTANCE: THE HOLY ROAD TO RESURRECTION

> For Christians, the ultimate meaning of life is Jesus Christ. The events of our personal and collective lives can only be understood in relationship to the life, death and resurrection of Jesus Christ.
> —John J. English, *Spiritual Freedom*

We often go through many stages of this healing journey at once. Or we zig and zag back and forth between stages. We don't have to figure things out or work hard to move from one stage to another. We just have to lovingly and prayerfully be with ourselves wherever we are.

In the section on the anger stage of forgiveness, I discussed a particularly painful wounding experience with a friend. When I look back over this time in my life, I see lots of fits and starts in healing. I would get better and forget about it, and then something would trigger the whole episode within me. I must freely admit that the mere passage of time seemed to help as much as anything else. I got a healthy perspective again. Other good things entered my life and reminded me of how blessed and fortunate I am.

I learned many lessons from the situation, including the ways in which my self-righteousness can irritate others. I can judge others and hurt them, no matter how callous or hardened (another judgment) they may appear to my eyes. I really wasn't a true friend to this person, either. It took a long time to admit these things to myself. I had to offer myself a lot of compassion before I trusted that I wouldn't lapse into self-hatred and harsh self-criticism.

I am embarrassed to offer this somewhat mild event as an example, considering the tough and wounding things that many people face in life. (Some of my friends wonder why I am driven to write about healing, when my own life has been so blessed. I freely admit it; it really has been blessed.) And yet, our inner journeys follow similar paths, regardless of the specifics of our situations. As my friend Paula D'Arcy says in her retreats, "Our pain is our pain. No one feels it as we do. Pain is pain, we needn't measure it or define it." We have to accept our challenges as *ours* for a reason.

There is no doubt that Jesus' acceptance in the garden led, in time, to his Resurrection. The suffering that came between the two events we know by heart. His entering into the very stuff of deep darkness led to new life. It is when we live our lives in awareness and courage as Jesus did that they become imbued with meaning. We are a resurrection people who pass through tomb times and grapple with darkness daily.

Author Joyce Rupp tells us that we must not romanticize this darkness. She says of herself that she loves the idea of standing outside when Jesus emerges from the tomb. But she does not relish going into the dark, dank and scary recesses of it. This, for all of us, is difficult. And yet the women of Jesus were fully prepared to do this very thing after they suffered with him at the foot of the cross. They knew what gave their lives meaning. If we don't fully enter our grief, it can become frozen and remain in the tombs of our hearts. Like Frank, we can enter a sort of living death.

When I move out of tomb-like depression and into acceptance, I find a dawning peace within myself. I want to do creative things again, and I feel hopeful and excited about the future. I want to work for Christ's kingdom. I forgive others easily. I can do tasks that require concentration. I laugh. I am more flexible and forgiving. People seem lovable again. I feel resurrected. Halleluiah!

FOR REFLECTION AND JOURNALING

+ Have there been those in your life you have reconciled with successfully? Write about this.
+ What times are tomb-like for you and how did you move out of them?
+ How do you feel when you are in acceptance and resurrection?
+ What brings acceptance into your life?

CLOSING PRAYER

I walked tomb-side with you Lord,
I dared to enter in. I felt the touch of darkness there,
But I felt new life stir in deep recesses of stone and light.
This is a mystery, but one that you know, Lord, so well.
Lead me through tomb darkness and into your light of love.
Amen.

Week Eleven: Day Six

THE RESURRECTION WALK

> But Mary stood weeping outside the tomb. As she wept,
> she bent over to look into the tomb; and she saw two
> angels in white, sitting where the body of Jesus had
> been lying, one at the head and the other at the feet.
> They said to her, "Woman, why are you weeping?" She
> said to them, "They have taken away my Lord, and I do
> not know where they have laid him." When she had
> said this, she turned around and saw Jesus standing
> there, but she did not know that it was Jesus. Jesus
> said to her, "Woman, why are you weeping? For whom
> are you looking?" Supposing him to be the gardener,
> she said to him, "Sir, if you have carried him away, tell
> me where you have laid him, and I will take him away."
> Jesus said to her, "Mary!" She turned and said to him
> in Hebrew, "Rabbouni!" (which means Teacher).
> —John 20:11–16

John sat in my office, filling the chair, a handsome man over six feet tall who looked as though he could walk onto a pro football team and catch a pass without any problem. He scraped his hand through his blonde hair as his eyes filled with tears. He wanted to share a resurrection moment with me.

"I responded to what you said about giving affirmations. That was really hard for my dad; he never said even that he loved me. Until the day I had to go away to Desert Storm. On that day, he said, 'John, I love you.'"

My eyes filled with tears also. I thought about the unnecessary suffering that we go through with one another. Here, a man whose father loved him dearly, but couldn't voice those feelings. Until the father said to himself, "I may never see this boy again. This may be my last chance."

In truth, we never know what tomorrow brings. Tomorrow may be too late to say I love you, and a resurrection moment will have passed us by. I was grateful that it had come for this man and his father. It had changed his life. Now John says, "I tell my children every day that I love them." As I sat there with him that day, I saw Christ truly risen in this man.

We may wonder how Mary could have mistaken Christ for the gardener. Richard Rohr explains, "True religion is radical, it cuts to the root of all (that we think we know). It moves us beyond our 'private I' and into reality.... Enlightenment is the great truth you know in a moment."[10]

Yet Mary's radical new vision took a little time to sink in. Her Lord lived? How could this be?

John Sanford tells us that Mary used a special word when she saw Jesus. *Rabbouni.* It is a word that approaches the meaning of *God.* She is seeing God emerge from the tomb.

Mary's reality was now being turned upon its head. Dead people do not rise again, yet life appeared in a new form, the resurrected life, filled with resurrection people. *Rabbouni, my Lord and my God!*

What is being resurrected within us now? What is there that is coming to life that we may not be able to recognize? Today we pray that God emerges from the tombs of our strivings, our depression and our falseness, and brings us new life. We are the life of God on this earth.

FOR REFLECTION AND JOURNALING
We are resurrected when...
+ We reach out to say, "I love you."

+ We really let something hurtful go, and we don't pick it up again.
+ We give freely without hope of recompense. We do small things with love.
+ We wake up to the *now*, and see the beauty that is all around us.
+ We are grateful for a hot cup of coffee or sunlight bouncing on a vase of flowers.
+ We ignore social standings and bank accounts in others.
+ We dare to use our gifts.
+ We give and receive loving or kind touch.
+ We welcome the stranger.

Journal as you wish. Would you like to sketch a resurrection morning?

CLOSING PRAYER

Now I step back and see the world and my place in it through large eyes...the eyes of the Risen One. It is Jesus, the Lord! Amen.

Week Eleven: Day Seven

ALLELUIA TIMES

It is important that we keep our eyes on the risen Lord. Here we see the hope of our lives. We too shall rise.
—M. Basil Pennington, *Seeking His Mind*

Prayer, touch, kindness, fragrance—all those things that live in rest and not in speed. Only when we take refuge in rest can we feel the company of angels that would minister to us....In the stillness there are forces and voices and hands and nourishment that arise, that

> take our breath away....This is what Jesus talks about
> when he speaks of the kingdom of God.
> —Wayne Muller, *Sabbath*

I have recently been doing a lot of work around the house. I have repainted some guests rooms and my office and cleared away a lot of junk. It feels really good to take things to Goodwill that I won't be using. It even feels good to throw away those old bills and circulars and stacks of catalogs that are cluttering my life.

We can de-clutter our lives if we want to. We can slow down and take some of the restlessness and the busyness out of them. We can learn to live without so much speed as we ask ourselves, "Do I really want to do this? Do I need to do this? Is it good for me or for others?" We can ask these questions when we are faced with one more of the activities that fill our busy lives.

It is in rest and reflection, in a meditative inner walk that we can live our alleluia season. We can take time to savor those things that take our breath away: a sunset splashed in oranges and pinks, a new grandchild in all her innocence, a simple, nourishing meal that is homemade. We call the voice of more, more, more to be still. We embrace what is, and we find it very good indeed.

FOR REFLECTION AND JOURNALING

How do you relate to resurrection time? Go through your prayer experiences for the week and see what God may be trying to teach you. Have some fun this week, dance with the Risen Christ; rejoice with him. What might be some enjoyable activities that you haven't considered doing for a while? Riding your bike or skating? Arranging flowers? Inviting friends over for a simple meal? Getting a massage?

And take some restful Sabbath time. Sit outside, or

near a window, and do nothing but *be.* Listen for the voices of the angels that say, "He is risen!"

CLOSING PRAYER
God, I am a pilgrim,
A pilgrim whose life does not depend
On reaching certain goals, but on being
Open to you, to hope, open to surprise, for you know
My way far better.
Than I do.
Amen.
—adapted from David Steindl-Rast, *Gratefulness, the Heart of Prayer*

Week Twelve

WELCOMING THE CALL OR RESISTING?

I see the paschal mystery constantly present in my life,
And in my resurrection time I hear your call.
You are calling me to something new, or the reworking of
what I do.
I know it.
And yet, I resist.
Change is uncomfortable for me.
I wonder why?
I wonder God, what you will do now?

Week Twelve: Day One

ARE YOU CALLING ME?

> Do not be afraid, Mary, for you have found favor with God.
> —Luke 1:30

> For at the core of the core of all creation flames the creative love of God, summoning out of chaos and nothingness all that exists, and lives, and comprehends.
> —Joseph A. Tetlow, *Choosing Christ in the World*

Our circular liturgical year spirals, leading us from the empty tomb through ordered time and back to the mysteries of Christ's birth. During the fall, I often have gatherings in my home to explore the spiritual journey. One evening we studied Lorenzo Monaco's painting, "The Annunciation." As we examined this extraordinary work, some participants observed that Mary seemed frightened. Others noticed that she was not turning toward the angel, but away. Others felt that Mary seemed to be making a decision, and that she might have been turning *toward* the angel as she spoke her "yes" to the voice of God. She is experiencing her great call. And we are called as well, by the one who created us.

We know that Mary faced uncertainty and fear as she was called to use her gifts in the world, indeed, to change her life. God was summoning new life out of chaos, and salvation was to come in all its mystery. It is the same with us—perhaps not in the size of the call but in the quality of the voice that calls us.

Healing our wounds is not just for ourselves alone. The voice of God comes to us in many forms, calling us to service in a life born again. Sometimes we welcome the voice. At other times it may cause us to be unsettled, frightened, resisting. In some ways that is the very reason I wrote this book. Do not be afraid.

FOR REFLECTION AND JOURNALING
+ Read the Luke text slowly and let it speak to your heart.
+ What changes are you experiencing that are causing you to turn toward God? Away from God?
+ Do you ever feel that life, or God, demands too much of you? Explain.
+ In what ways are your special gifts calling out to you?

CLOSING PRAYER
My soul proclaims the greatness of my God,
And my spirit can rejoice in God my Savior.
For he has looked upon his lowly one with favor,
And blessed is his name. Amen.

Week Twelve: Day Two
BEGINNING TO HEAR THE CALL WITH TENDERNESS

A significant shift of functional identity slowly stirs within us. We're less the teacher, the computer programmer, the nurse, the physician—and more the celebrant of tenderness. Instead of reacting to persons and things around us, we respond to the tender Presence that sustains them and sustains us.
—Brennan Manning, *The Wisdom of Tenderness*

I begin now by suggesting that all people have callings. Everyone. We are all on earth with special duties. No exceptions. You are here for a reason. A very important reason. You have neither the right nor the powers to

have someone else make your contributions. If you do
not live out your calling, the calling will go forever
unanswered.

—Robert J. Furey, *Called by Name*

The time was the summer of 1995, and I sat in Cincinnati's
downtown square near its magnificent fountain *Genius of
the Waters,* a work of art exhibiting all our uses of water
from agriculture to medicine to exploration. The *Genius*
was unconcerned that day, continuing to pour out her benef-
icence upon all the earth as I scribbled relentlessly in my
journal. The call to use my creative gifts had risen, no
longer to be denied in my life. I was attending a National
Pastoral Musicians convention, and every day at noon I
would walk the few blocks to this square, munch on a hamburger, and try to make sense of my inner life. I was overcoming the wound of low self-esteem in my life that had
kept me so frozen. I was being loved out of it by my friends,
by happy circumstance, by God.

I had brought with me an original liturgical recording.
Seven songs! But how to give them to anyone? How to face
the fear of condescending smirks, dismissive gestures? How
to release my pearls without getting trampled down? I
feared for my creative life. I feared that too much discouragement would send me forever packing, burying my gifts
ever deeper, all the while denying my pain with a toothy
smile. I was so good at *that.* I wasn't as good at taking creative risks.

As the sun shone down and the jugglers celebrated in
the square, I daily began to release my fears. Something felt
right. I was *here at this very place for a reason.* Tenderness
and love filled me and crowded out my fear. A presence was
ordering my steps.

FOR REFLECTION AND JOURNALING

+ List what you believe are your special gifts. Don't discount small things, like being able to fix a car or bake a cake.
+ Do you believe that God has a plan for your special gifts? Why?

CLOSING PRAYER

My soul proclaims the greatness of my God,
And my spirit can rejoice in God my Savior.
For he has looked upon his lowly one with favor,
And blessed is his name. Amen.

Week Twelve: Day Three

ANGELS ALONG THE WAY

> To give up asking God for help may mean we are losing confidence in God or in ourselves. Or maybe we are beginning to lose sight of our dependence on God. The Holy Spirit praying in us will give us the power to persevere in our requests and to purify our trust in our Father.
> —Arthur Baranowski, *Praying Alone and Together*

> ...look for someone willing to teach you without controlling you...find someone who will help you lead yourself. In other words, find someone who won't block your view of God by pretending to be God.
> —Robert J. Furey, *Called by Name*

When I finally ventured out over the vast National Pastoral Musicians convention exhibit area to share my recording with some editor who might like it, I covered myself with a mantle of affirmation and prayer. I never stopped praying. I had practically memorized the book *The Artist's Way*. I repeated affirmations; I *believed* that somehow God would help me. I wandered into a booth and met Mark Bernard. a young man who was to become a mentor for me. Mark was heading up a new liturgical arm for a well-known musical press, and I just struck up a conversation with him. A broad discussion of liturgical music led to the discussion of the music I had written. I was so excited that Mark was willing to listen to some of it and see if it could be published by his company. We went on to form a professional relationship and his publisher, Unity, published three of my songs. One of them, "My Jesus Walked," received a lot of affirming attention and had respectable sales. I will always be grateful to Mark for his faith in my work. And although our lives have moved in different directions, the memory remains of his angelic presence in my life. I have moved on to my true gift, which is writing books. And I built my writing career, at least in part, on the foundation of affirmation that Mark gave me.

FOR REFLECTION AND JOURNALING

+ Who affirms you and values your gifts?
+ Do you mentor anyone?
+ What makes you fearful of using your gifts?

CLOSING PRAYER

I thank you that you call me,
And place those in my life who encourage me.
Bless you, Lord, and bless them! Amen.

Week Twelve: Day Four

BUT IT'S SO HARD TO CHANGE!

> ...we went through fire and through water;
> yet you have brought us out to a spacious place.
> —Psalm 66:12

I once worked at school with Laurie, a talented and kind kindergarten teacher who had to seek therapy because her depression threatened to overwhelm her life. She was surprised that the therapist quickly asked that she change many of her own behaviors. She was the mother of two small children and had a husband whom she described as demanding. Laurie found it easier just to do everything around the house herself: cleaning, bathing the children and even mowing the lawn. All this effort combined with her challenging job had left her depleted. Ethan, her therapist, told her it was little wonder that she was depressed!

He advised her to draw up a list of chores and divide them up. He told her that even her seven year old could make her bed and take her towels to the laundry room. Laurie was to ask her husband to clean the kitchen after supper (as a first step!), and she was not to take over if the job didn't get done.

As Laurie struggled to implement these changes, she told me that she thought the purpose of therapy was, "to help me cope with my life better. I didn't know that I would have to change, and that my family would start hating me! They just adored me before!"

Laurie had not yet realized that she was answering God's call: a call to use her time, talents and energy in life-giving ways. A call to change for herself and for others.

It was small wonder that these changes disrupted the life that Laurie and her family had grown accustomed to. In her book *Heart of Flesh,* Joan Chittister advises us that Christian humility should be practiced by all, that when one member of the family or group does all the submission and service to others, it become oppression, not humility. Perhaps Laurie's family didn't mean to take advantage of her. They exhibited the human propensity to sin and selfishness that we all have. The changes in their lives threatened them and made them fearful that Laurie was changing too much. The ground was shifting under their feet. And yet, let us be clear. Laurie was called to change. Laurie *had* to change to live her life with authenticity.

Resistance without and within will occur at its highest level when we are experiencing the most growth in our souls. As you take continue to journey with this book, be alert to the movements within and without you. Notice both your inner resistance to change and the resistance of those around you. Be reluctant to share your stories with those who need much healing themselves.

FOR REFLECTION AND JOURNALING

+ How do you feel about Laurie's experience? Do you relate to it? In what ways?
+ Does anyone feel threatened by healing changes in your life? Explain.
+ What is calling out for change and growth in your life? In what ways do you need to set boundaries so that your call can be realized?

CLOSING PRAYER

Why do I resist your workings in my life,
When what you do is good and you are all good?
Draw me close again, and give me courage.
Through change and even crisis, you are there.
Like Peter on the water, I sink only
When I take my eyes off your face.
Amen.

Week Twelve: Day Five

OVERCOMING NEGATIVITY WHEN ANSWERING THE CALL

> Then they arrived at the country of the Gerasenes,
> which is opposite Galilee. As he stepped out on land, a
> man of the city who had demons met him. For a long
> time he had worn no clothes, and he did not live I a
> house but in the tombs.
> —Luke 8:26–27

This seems like a scary story. Not only is this man possessed, but he comes to Jesus *out of the tombs*, a place of spirits and hauntings. Jesus is unimpressed and sends the demons packing, out into a herd of pigs and down to destruction.

I find the term *demon* useful in my own life. The negative forces within me can seem like demons, virulent beings beyond my control. When I first began to write seriously, I had to contend with deeply placed and vicious negative voices within. These voices tried a number of approaches to keep me from writing. They told me that I had other jobs I should be doing, usually things like organizing drawers or folding clothes. If that failed, they told me that I was wasting my time, that no one would read what I wrote. They told me that many, many others knew a lot more about spirituality that I did, and that they were the ones who were entitled to write about it. It took a lot of energy, getting help, and praying to rise above these voices enough to write on a regular basis.

They are voices of ego-fear. Julia Cameron says, "Most of the time when we are blocked in an area of our life, it is because we feel safer that way. We may not be happy, but at least we know what we are—unhappy. Much fear of our own creativity is the fear of the unknown."[11]

I also see my demons in my driving need to fix situations, my unkindness to myself when I make mistakes, my relentless ambition, and my quick reactions to what others say. My unreasonable anger when I have been hurt can be demonic. (Usually, it is turned inward.) The part of my mind that sometimes judges others and myself and finds us all not up to standards (whose?) is a destructive little devil. Well, I could go on, but you may understand all too well. You may have similar demons within you. Most are enemies of the call and cause us to resist the workings of grace.

This passage illustrates that Jesus is not afraid of our demons, our weakness, our sins, the negative voices that we experience so painfully. He doesn't turn away in disgust or disbelief that we could be so sinful and broken after all this time. He is there to heal and to love us to greater health and to help us get our demons under control.

FOR REFLECTION AND JOURNALING

+ Do you relate to the word *demon*? How do you feel about the way Jesus handles these demons?
+ In what ways are you continuing to long for God's healing and inspiration?
+ Write a counter argument to what the negative voices may be saying within you.

CLOSING PRAYER

Help me Lord,
I round the corner,
there they are
I wash the dishes,
there they are.
But especially when I try to answer your call,
there they are—so many
negative voices in my heart.

Take them over for me, throw them out for me,
as you did the demons so long ago.
and I will make my heart a home
for you alone. Amen.

Week Twelve: Day Six

THE CHRIST OF FAILURE

> May I never boast of anything except the cross of our
> Lord Jesus Christ....
> —Galatians 6:14

I stand in the sunlight and gaze at etchings that were
placed on rugged rock fifteen hundred years ago, brown surface chipped away to reveal cream beneath. Dancing war-
riors. Hallowed spirals. Sheep or goat-like animals sought
in the sacred hunt. Around me is the stillness of the desert,
the lifted arms of the sequoia, the muted rustle of tiny
rodents and the watery song of nearby birds.

I am attending a Catholic Writers' conference at Picture
Rocks near Tucson, Arizona. I have had ample time to meditate upon God's call. Now I think, *No wonder we resist it.
The way it tears at us.* I had forgotten the angst that is present at writing conferences. I had forgotten the writer's
question, "Why did God put this desire to write in my heart
when it is so hard? When there is no success, no way to get
my word out? Why must I turn myself inside out to get
these words if no one cares to hear them?"

The pain of the not published was weighing upon my
heart. I remembered it clearly, painfully. I wanted to put my
arms around each writer and say, "There, there. It will be all
right. Don't give up hope. Go gently, now." My mind churned.
I wondered which of the group would persevere and which

would fall away, not to hear the call again. In the end, I knew, most would continue to write because they had to.

Major resistance to the call comes midway when things don't turn out the way we had planned. Things just get too hard. We find nothing in our work that could reasonably be called success yet we continue to be driven by the same call. We know that this call comes from core desire, yet we don't understand the ways that our ministry is playing out in the world.

Turning away now from the picture rocks, I walk into the Way of the Cross that is gently laid out in the desert landscape. I make the journey to each station. "There is little in the walk of Jesus that could have been called success," I think, just as so many in ministries don't taste much of what the world calls success.

There is Evelyn, who worked for her parish for fifteen years at tiny wages and in every capacity and is summarily let go when a new priest arrives. There is Mia, who stands up for the poor in her community and is branded as odd and "just a hippie." There is the deacon in my parish, who struggles to run a small business, pay his bills and be a husband and father. He works tirelessly for the church at the same time, sometimes feeling he fails at everything.

I know of the mother and father who, as they bail their child out of jail, wonder what went so terribly wrong. The face of each is the face of the unsuccessful Jesus. In some paradoxical way, those of us seeking gospel life are called to what most would call failure.

We each must find within our own hearts what the gospel life calls us to. I turn back to the Stations of the Cross. At this moment it is clear that I wander in a desert landscape and that Jesus falls and falls again. I bow my head and with the most heartfelt emotion I pray.

FOR REFLECTION AND JOURNALING

+ How does failure haunt your calling? Does it discourage you? Write about this.

+ How can failure contain the seeds of a better tomorrow, as you walk in your calling?

CLOSING PRAYER

Is it true, my dear Jesus?
That my failures are as dear to you as my successes? Perhaps more dear?
I hardly dare believe it. And yet your desert times teach me, your way of cross declares to me,
that this is true.
Let me understand this, live it,
and even cherish it.
Amen.

Week Twelve: Day Seven

CALLED AND CHOSEN

> What if people really are called to certain tasks? What if all those self-help books are wrong about how we are in complete control of our destinies? What if each and every one of us has his or her own mission (or set of missions) and right path in life? What if we have callings but miss them? What if we miss them because we never listened hard enough?
> —Robert J. Furey, *Called by Name*

Sometimes I believe God uses the call in my life simply to give me joy. There are days when I don't want to go to either choir practice or to Mass where we sing. I don't want to go because I am tired, bummed out or slightly ill. And yet, when I go (because I really do have to) I always end up feeling better: more joyful, more hopeful and less fearful. I connect with the small community of the choir, and I connect with the hopeful message of the words we are singing. And so in an odd paradoxical way, the fruit of my call is not just for community, but for me as well.

FOR REFLECTION AND JOURNALING

+ As you look back over your journaling for the week, consider your special gifts and callings. Do you feel connected to using your gifts in God's kingdom while you take care of yourself? How do you do this now? What resistance might prevent your doing so?

CLOSING PRAYER

To me, the very least of the holy ones,
The power was given: to preach the inscrutable riches of
    Christ,
And to bring light for all,
This is the plan of the mystery hidden from all ages past,
In God who created all things.
—adapted from Ephesians 3:8–9

Week Thirteen

THE CALL: LEARNING TO LOVE AS GOD LOVES

In fits and starts,
I am overcoming my resistance
to answering God's call
and knowing myself as holy and whole,
completely suited to do God's work in this world.
I don't have to be perfect
or bigger than life.
I just have to be and accept
(wonder of wonders!)
myself,
created, ah yes,
in God's image.
You show me my weaknesses and strengths,
my sins and glories,
and all is well
In you.

Week Thirteen: Day One

MULTIPLYING THE LOAVES

> The whole Christian Community is filled with the
> Spirit of Jesus, whose guidance inspires every new
> initiative, and who ensures the harmony of the early
> community in its prayer, joy and praise. Even
> persecution brings only joy and thanksgiving.
> —*The Jerusalem Bible,* Commentary on Acts of the
> Apostles

> Remember two things about love: First, love is action,
> not talk; it shows itself in the deed done, not simply in
> words spoken. Second, love works itself out in mutual
> sharing, so that the lover always gives to and receives
> from the beloved—everything: gifts, money, convictions,
> honors, position....I want to have an intimate
> understanding of myself and my life as gift.
> —Joseph A. Tetlow, *Choosing Christ in the World*

> And all ate and were filled. What was left over was
> gathered up, twelve baskets of broken pieces.
> —Luke 9:17

Let me tell you a true tale.

Once upon a time there was a remnant tribe of one hundred Africans who faced starvation after being pushed off their grazing lands during civil war. Far away, in a little south Louisiana town, a Catholic schoolteacher read of their plight. The article she read had been written by a former student of hers, now living in Atlanta, who worked with one of the tribe's relatives.

The teacher, Mrs. Bourgeoisie, read the article to her fifth grade students. The tribe needed ten thousand dollars to relocate and grow crops! The children asked, "Can *we* help?" The boys and girls brought in their pennies and dimes and dollars. They had to earn all the money, not ask their parents for it. They wrote letters to the tribe telling them about giving up money earmarked for a new ball glove, or babysitting all weekend and then donating the money. They prayed for the endangered people in the tribe.

The lady who had originally written the article received their money (two hundred dollars) and the letters written by the children. They were the only ones who had responded to her plea! Her mood changed from despair to hope as she read the letters written by the fifth grade students. Inspired by the letters, she and her friends walked door to door in their affluent Atlanta neighborhood and asked for donations, showing those they encountered the letters. When their neighbors read what children had done, they gave also. A benefit concert was held. When the money was all counted, the group raised the ten thousand dollars, and one hundred lives and probably more, considering babies on the way, were saved.

I heard about this tale because I know the compassionate teacher in this story. She comes to me for spiritual direction, but I often feel I should sit on the other side of the table! She smiles as she tells the story and ends it in this way, "And this, Lyn, was the multiplication of the loaves and the fishes."

We too often abandon the call because we think we can't possibly make a difference in this old sad world of ours, yet we can. We offer what we have freely, and Christ multiplies it... again and again.

FOR REFLECTION AND JOURNALING
+ What is the nature of the call in your life now?

+ What small steps could you take to answer the call of Christ?
+ Reflect on the blessings in your life. How can you multiply them by focusing on what you have rather than on what you lack?

CLOSING PRAYER

God, what work are you putting plainly in my sight?
What work for your kingdom of light? Amen.

Week Thirteen: Day Two

WHO ME? MOSES?

> Then I consider and ponder this, that God remains present in every moment to every creature. God stays there always sustaining existence, and life and reflection.
> —Joseph A. Tetlow, *Choosing Christ in the World*

> Fire is a manifestation of God. As eternal fire, God appears in the burning bush as later Spirit would appear at Pentecost as tongues of fire.
> —Mariann Burke, *Advent and Psychic Birth*

Once, before I started to write for publication, I was attending a Paula D'Arcy retreat on the grounds of St. Charles College in Grand Coteau. I arose very early one beautiful fall morning and walked the handsome grounds and pastures around the retreat center.

As I arrived at the cemetery, I saw it. I saw a burning bush! The rising sun illuminated an azalea bush with an incredibly rich, blazing, liquid red light. The bush burned, lit as if from within by Spirit's light. I stood there for many minutes and thought of Moses and the call and my own life.

What do I know about you, God, I thought, *that I can speak of you to others? What if they ask me your name; what will I say? Will I say that you called* my *name from a burning bush on an October day near a cemetery?*

I can tell you with authority that the call comes in many ways if we are open and look with new eyes. I haven't thought about the burning bush and that conversation with God for a long time. I didn't know that I would try to tell others God's name or speak of Spirit in many ways. We answer the call by doing the next thing and the next thing. Doors don't open until we are ready to walk through them. This is faith.

And so, dear friends, if you ask me God's name today, I will tell it to you. It is Love.

FOR REFLECTION AND JOURNALING

+ Look for the call in your life, hidden in the ordinariness of each day.
+ What have been some times when you encountered the burning bush?

CLOSING PRAYER

Create your own prayer. Write it down!

Week Thirteen: Day Three

STAR CHILDREN

> Could it be that our bodies are simply light's radiation locus throughout the years of our life and that, because of that, we truly are "children of the Light"?—Is consciousness the "light" gift that we bring to our sojourn here on earth?—Are we perhaps temples of light?
>
> —Barbara Fiand, *In the Stillness You Will Know*

> "Look towards heaven and count the stars, if you are able to count them." Then he said to him, "So shall your descendants be."
> —Genesis 15:5

Scientists tell us that each of us contain atoms of stars that lived thousands of years ago. We are a part of the stars and the stars are a part of us. We are interconnected with all that has been and all that will be, in a dance of covenant love with the creator of all that is. This covenant was illustrated in God's promise to Abraham: Your descendants will be like the stars in the heaven.

To celebrate this covenant, a child would be born to Sarah. She would birth the promise of the covenant. The coming of a child to the aged is a theme that is found throughout Jewish/Christian Scripture; just when all hope is gone, hope of new life is realized. As a woman who has battled with infertility, I can relate closely to this struggle of the Hebrew women of old. They longed for the children of their hearts. And we long for the new birth today, the refreshing of tired hearts and minds.

We are renewed when we remember that God is the hungry lover, roaming the earth, looking for those who will love him back. God keeps doing the new thing, bringing the new child into our midst, surprising us with the extent of his seeking, covenant love. He whispers again and again that we are his children, children of the stars.

Because of the covenant, we are called to shine forth as stars of hope for the world. We are no longer to hide our light under baskets, but to bravely walk forth, carrying the light.

FOR REFLECTION AND JOURNALING

+ In what way are you a star of light? In what way do you feel God as the hungry lover, searching for you? In what ways might this message fall coldly upon your heart?

+ How do you want to live out your call to covenant, family of God, love?

CLOSING PRAYER

O, Lord, you search me and you know me.
You are wondrous, Lord,
And all your works are wondrous.
They are as numerous and beautiful as the stars.
And I am a star in your heaven.
I shine with your light. Amen.

Week Thirteen: Day Four

BARRIERS AND BRIDGES: MARTY AND FATHER MISTAKEN

> Lord, mighty God, in power and wisdom you shape me
> and my life and world—my time, my city, my language.
> You give me understanding and passions—You give me
> voice to sing songs to You for all creation. For all that
> has passed between us, I thank You.
> —Joseph A. Tetlow, *Choosing Christ in the World*

> We seek to be governed by a spirit of truth, and truth,
> we know is light. Being guided into the truth can be a
> devastating experience.
> —Joan Puls, *Seek Treasures in Small Fields*

> As I finally got to the bottom of my feelings of despair, I
> realized I did not have to run from them; they were a
> part of me, but they did not have to have the last word.
> In time, I came to appreciate the great wealth hidden
> in my suffering.
> —Phillip Bennett, *Let Yourself Be Loved*

Marty loved music before he could walk. By the time he was
sixteen and had reached the seminary, his guitar was his
core passion. While others prayed and meditated, Marty hid

behind the velvety curtains in the auditorium and played his guitar because he was not allowed to play at Mass, no matter how much he was called to do so. It wasn't done then. No guitars allowed!

He was close to a certain priest who shared his love of music, Father Mistaken. Sometimes Marty and Father would sit in Father's office and listen to jazz or classical tapes and discuss them. Marty felt that this man understood his core passion. He discovered that before Father Mistaken had become a priest he was a drummer in a band, years and years ago.

One day Father Mistaken found Marty behind the velvet curtains when he was supposed to be at Vespers. In a stunning reversal of attitude, he marched Marty back to the dormitory and proceeded to throw everything Marty owned on the floor, as boys returning from Vespers watched in wonder. Raging, Father Mistaken hurtled books and papers, clothes and toiletries onto the floor. He actually took Marty's bed apart and tumbled the mattress against a wall. Then he said, "All you care about is that damn guitar." In his heart, Marty answered, "You may be right."

Was the shadow of Father Mistaken (his own frustrated desire to play music) the tyrant that showed up and destroyed Marty's room? Marty will never know because, not surprisingly, Marty soon left the seminary. He became a well-known blues and jazz guitarist and toured widely, playing to large audiences all over the south. He cut records and backed up some of the biggest names in the music business. Marty also made a lot of choices that weren't life-giving. At times he lived so close to the edge it was a wonder that he didn't fall to his destruction. There were times he faced despair and loneliness so great that it threatened to have the last word in his life. Yet in a paradoxical way, all that had been a barrier became a bridge to his new life.

I will fast-forward this recording to its climax: Thirty years after hiding behind auditorium curtains, Marty faced a simple congregation at St. Michael's Church as he prepared to play and sing for the 9:00 A.M. liturgy. He said, "I have played for auditoriums filled with thousands of people, but I was never as nervous as I was that day." Marty doesn't take the Mass for granted. It is a newly recovered gift in his life, as is the community he now claims as his own.

How has he arrived here? If you ask Marty, he will tell you about the compassionate priest who listened to his general confession for most of a day and told Marty that God was setting him free from his past, all of the past. A great healing occurred in Marty's life that day.

He might even mention my name because I have been directing him in the nineteenth annotation for many months. We have become brother and sister in Spirit.

But mostly Marty will tell you of the voice of Love that never left him during all those years that he ran, and ran faster. Finally returning to a flawed and human church, he embraces his own humanity. He brings his guitar with him and he brings his own flaws and wounds as well as his sparkling gifts. He stumbles as he tries to understand his call. He is just like the rest of us. And I believe that God looks with love and sees that it is good.

For Reflection and Journaling
+ You may want to journal in response to this story, or similar happenings in your own life.
+ How have overly authoritarian figures impacted your growth, if at all?

Closing Prayer
Homecomings.
The lost sheep, Lord,
Are always stumbling home.

They didn't find perfection anywhere!
The greener grass was a mirage,
The beckoning waters were suited for drowning.
And you, flawed and risen church,
You, glorious and hurting church,
Do you need us as we need you?
Did we ask too much, or give too little?
The questions of your sheep echo
Through the rolling chasms of change that surely
must come
Everywhere.
Amen.

Week Thirteen: Day Five

LIVING THE CALL WITH ONE ANOTHER

> The daily dance of love cannot be learned ahead of
> time, the steps must be taken one at a time. The dance
> cannot be rushed; it has its own pace. As we dance, we
> find ourselves surrounded by love. An unexpected
> person, event, or insight transforms the whole day and
> we see the world with new eyes.
> —Phillip Bennett, *Let Yourself Be Loved*

For many years our nephew Paul longed for a loving marriage as he battled serious illness, then recovered. We loved him dearly, and longed for him to find peace and happiness. We thought he had realized his dreams when he married in 1996. However, the marriage lasted only months, leaving Paul broken and depressed. He lost his job at about the same time. Paul lived in another state, and we and his sisters worried deeply about him and talked to him for hours on the telephone.

"He's such a sweet guy," we said to one another, "Why is he having such a hard time?" In a suffering world, we stumble about with our questions, "Why? Why?" I don't ask this question as much as I used to, I just watch; I practice awareness. Often answers don't come; but sometimes they do. These are not answers that explain suffering. They are answers that say, "Yes, there is suffering, but something else is coming. Pay attention, this is next."

Paul got a new job and moved to Oklahoma. One day in a Chinese restaurant he met an Asian woman named Lily who had been in the United States for two years. Paul felt love immediately, but he held back cautiously. After a courtship of about a year, Lily and Paul married. They are very happy indeed. Paul and Lily are called to live their call in family. They have both overcome tremendous obstacles to do this thing which so many take for granted. They live their call with one another.

They visited us at Christmas, and to see them together was pure joy. Each had been lonely until Spirit brought them together. Their relationship is marked with gratitude, lightness of spirit, and mutual affection.

Paul is now forty-nine and Lily is approaching forty. I got an E-mail from them recently: Lily is expecting a baby! They are ecstatic! Although they both wanted a family passionately, they had not been at all confident that Lily would conceive at her age. My husband and I immediately thought, "Paul will be almost seventy when this child graduates from high school!" We didn't express this thought to Paul, but I am sure he would say, "God has brought us this far; he will see us through." (Oh, ye of little faith!)

Lily...and Mary and Elizabeth of Luke's Gospel. All blessed with unexpected children. One of my first thoughts upon hearing about Lily's pregnancy was, "I wonder if she is past her third month?" We women know that after the third month, a pregnancy is deemed more secure and its loss less likely. Often a woman is sick during the first three months and feels better as she enters her fourth and fifth months of pregnancy. She finds her energy again and prepares enthusiastically for her child.

I was blessed with a deeper meaning, therefore, upon rereading Luke's text of the Visitation. I realized that Mary stayed with Elizabeth for three months. Mary arrived at Elizabeth's soon after the Annunciation that marked the beginning of her own pregnancy. How appropriate, I thought. Elizabeth was in her sixth month when Mary arrived, and was feeling stronger, healthier and more secure. Elizabeth could offer the young girl consolation and companionship during the early months of Mary's pregnancy. Perhaps she said, "My pregnancy is turning out well, Mary, and yours will also. We are so blessed!"

I can visualize them chatting about their children as they stitched tiny garments from textured linen. Just as women have done through the ages, they shared their hopes, their fears, their love, blessing one another with relationship and a communal journey. I am sure they sought the meaning and depth of their experiences as they murmured over their bread in the soft morning light or washed the supper plates. They lived their call with one another, supporting one another in family, in community.

When I first began to write this story, Lily hadn't quite made it to her third month. She was sick daily, dear lady, but I have always been told that this is a sign of a strong pregnancy. So in phone calls we shared encouraging words with Paul.

Lily doesn't speak a lot of English, but Paul passed our love along to her. In relationship we tell our stories, sing our songs. We support one another and the meaning of our lives becomes clearer. Like Mary and Elizabeth we celebrate the unexpected joys and challenges of all our days.

(Note: Joseph Li Lormand came into the world on December 28, 2003, with all ten fingers and toes and lots of black hair. Now his father walks the floor at night with a moist little sleepy person on his shoulder. Lily sleeps when she can, and feels like she nurses much of the rest of the time! They tell us that life is good, and they will come to Louisiana to christen the baby in March. We can't wait to see him. A gift. A blessing. A new member of our family in Christ.)

FOR REFLECTION AND JOURNALING

+ Write any reflections you have on this story.
+ What events in your life are surprising you with joy?
+ Who shares your work in Christ with you?
+ Recall a time in your past when things seemed very dark, and then turned around. Where was God in this event?

CLOSING PRAYER

God, for this one day,
Let the world turn.
And take away my sorrow.
Let the world turn.
Bringing joy's hidden face,
Laughter once unheard...

Week Thirteen: Day Six

Six days later, Jesus took with him Peter and James
and John, and led them up a high mountain apart, by

themselves. And he was transfigured before them, and
his clothes became dazzling white, such as no one on
earth could bleach them. . . . Then Peter said to Jesus,
"Rabbi, it is good for us to be here; let us make three
dwellings...."
—Mark 9:2–3, 5

On this day, it would be good for you to remember some
mountaintop experiences in your life. Perhaps these came
when you were truly living your call, whether in marriage
and family or in your vocation. Perhaps you were on retreat
or participating in an unusually moving Mass or prayer
service. At these times, our hearts seem to be transfigured,
we feel the presence of God, close to us, enlivening us and
filling us with his Spirit.

It is good to remember these times as we persevere on
this journey of prayer. We may be fatigued as we approach
the end of this book. Discouragement may come and go. The
dailiness of our lives can seem endless. When we feel like
this, the consolation of mountaintop experiences can return
and console us. We can't build our homes on the mountain-
tops, but we can remember their lofty heights with love.

For Reflection and Journaling
Write about some of your peak spiritual experiences. If you
are led to, you may want to paint them, write a poem about
them, make a collage, or just journal in depth about them.
Allow yourself to relive the joy of these experiences.

Closing Prayer
Jesus, you were transfigured on the mountaintop, and we
saw clearly your holy face. At times I have been transfigured by your love. Help me to remember those times now
and rejoice again in them. Amen.

Week Thirteen: Day Seven

LEARNING TO LOVE AS GOD LOVES

> Blessed are those who have not seen, and yet come to believe.
> —John 20:29b

> Groping in the dark, witness to unfathomable truths, the soul gathers strength. One still cannot see, but sight is not important now. All that is important is given.
> —Beverly Lanzetta, *Path of the Heart*

As long as we live on this earth, we will not see everything clearly. Therefore, it seems difficult to love as God loves. It seems hard to be that loving at all! I think the secret is that we *are* given all that is important to this quest. We are given what we need to become conduits for grace. What is required is removing that within us which blocks the flow of grace, or rather we ask God to remove those things within us.

We may need to continue to ask that our egos be quieted and learn humility. We may ask that our fear be softened yet again. Trust may need building within us, and, if so, we should continue to pray for that growing trust. Our impatience or our judgments about others may be blocking our love. Let us pray that God will correct these things within us and make us more compassionate.

As we live our calling with love, be it in family, church, business place, theater, art gallery or school, we seek to open our hearts more and to listen intently to what God is telling us. Discernment comes as we slow down, pay attention and listen. As we do this, we know what to do: this person needs a word of affirmation; this person needs my full attention, *now*; I need to complete this task before there are negative consequences.

Or we hear within our hearts: you need to rest; you're doing too much. We even find ourselves being led to certain places at certain times. Our lives take on a sort of magical quality as we listen, listen, listen. Even though we only see a tiny patch of the road ahead, we can be at peace. The love of God fills us and makes us whole.

FOR REFLECTION AND JOURNALING

+ What graces do you pray for today?
+ What impediments to grace within yourself would you like to remove?
+ Are you able to listen closely to what God may be telling you?
+ What would it mean to you to love as God loves?

CLOSING PRAYER

When we know the seasons of things, we can feel their timing, their readiness. There is less pushing, more waiting to see what is necessary.
—Wayne Muller, *Sabbath*

Lord, you guide me to what is necessary, I don't need to push,
In my work, my home, my life.
I need only open myself to the call, to love as you love,
Without condition, without fear.
Let things come in their season. Let my heart be filled with readiness.
I will slow down, I will look, I will listen with tenderness.
Let me love, oh let me love as you do.
Amen.

Week Fourteen

LIVING WITH GOD PRESENT NOW

What would it mean to be healed enough,
To be courageous enough
to live the call?
What would that look like; how would I do it?
What have others found?
The call lived in wholeness
Is blessed. This I feel for sure.

Week Fourteen: Day One

THE LIGHT WITHIN

> There is a piece of light in all of us,
> Maybe hidden or buried with pain
> Perhaps pushed in the corner by shame—
> Seen or unseen the light is there.
> —Joyce Rupp, *The Cosmic Dance*

> Blessed are the poor in spirit, for theirs is the kingdom
> of heaven.
> —Matthew 5:3

It was a magical weekend at Our Lady of the Oaks in Grand Coteau. I don't remember the weather, but I remember the wonderful women who sat, so open and rapt, so lovingly listening to me as I reached out to them. I fell in love with them, and they loved me back. It was a Christ-love flowing among us. Nothing mattered but this love; our sizes and shapes, colors, wealth, poverty or status didn't seem important. We were naked souls, I guess, living for a time in a soul-space. That is the best way I can describe it.

After the retreat, as I read through my evaluations one struck me forcibly. It contained a truth, and one that I had not articulated to myself. The woman wrote: *When Lyn Doucet speaks to us, there seems to be a light within her.*

I was filled with awe, humility and gratitude. Yes, I had felt this, this warm and invigorating light, the source of *inspiration.* It was Spirit and love. It flowed through my healed and grateful heart as *the women on retreat* gave it to me. They were Jesus to me. I believe that Christ had come that weekend to be with us in a special way. We saw God clearly, shining in one another.

Sometimes when we are truly living God's call in our lives, we finally get beyond ourselves. Totally gone is our striving ego and our chattering mind, at least for a time. We are in the flow of doing God's work, and we feel it.

This does not mean that struggle goes and remains away. It returns, and so does confusion at times. There are days when I fear my light has gone out. Yet we remember those times of sweet consolation, of living in spirit, and they keep us on the right road.

FOR REFLECTION AND JOURNALING

+ Think back to times that you felt truly inspired...filled with Spirit. Write about these times.
+ With whom do you share Christ-love, a love that is all-embracing and unconditional?

CLOSING PRAYER

Come, Holy Spirit.
Enliven our hearts and our minds. Amen.

Week Fourteen: Day Two

TAKING UP OUR PERSONAL CROSSES

> If any want to become my followers, let them deny themselves and take up their cross and follow me. For those who want to save their life will lose it, and those who lose their life for my sake will find it.
> —Matthew 16:24–25

I have been told by people all my life that I remind them of Carol Burnett. Others say, *no way!* but the comments keep coming. Occasionally, I remind people of Mary Tyler Moore, and I like that better. But no, Carol Burnett is what I usually hear.

Part of the reminder is my appearance (big smile, lots of teeth that are barely contained after years of braces)...but a large part of the resemblance is my laughter and my joke-telling which bubbles up easily and often. This humor is a natural gift from my dad, who loves to laugh and relishes a good story.

This aspect of my persona came up after I had directed a lady named Susan for about a year. She and I met her sister Janie for lunch. Over stretchy-cheesy Italian creations at the local sandwich shop, Janie remarked that she would like to go to "a happy spiritual director" like Susan had. I smiled at the compliment. Then Susan pointed a backward thumb at me and said to Janie, "You know what Carol Burnett here said? She said the daily cross she takes up is *herself!*"

Laughter all around. I smiled with them, but I couldn't deny the truth of it. The daily cross I take up is living in this middle-aged body, in this place, with my impediments and humanness. The daily cross is striving to do God's work with my moodiness, over-sensitivity, easy fatigue, selfishness, and a certain amount of unconsciousness that will probably not completely go away and slaps me in the face periodically. It hurts every time.

My cross is the call to live as Christ in the world with nothing but the tools I have been given, relying almost totally on grace to make it come out right. My cross is that I will never live like Christ all that well, but I must keep trying.

I believe that healing and conversion must occur so that we can have the courage to even begin to live out our call. But healing will never be complete on this side of the heavens. The struggle with our false selves, our egos and our demons will play out in a dying and rising that will continue as we live out the call. Yet, we mustn't give up. We have to keep on loving ourselves and others. And to all this I can only say: Your will be done, God. Alleluia, Amen.

FOR REFLECTION AND JOURNALING
+ How do you live out your call today?
+ What aspects of the cross, as revealed in this story, do you still struggle with?

CLOSING PRAYER
Oh Lord, you know me well, and you still love me so much.
God, you made me as I am and you form me each moment.
Let me cherish who I am, in all humility,
As I live the gospel call every day. Amen.

Week Fourteen: Day Three
ROLLING BACK THE STONE

> Suppose we were able to put aside our dominant
> experience of fear and let ourselves instead to be taken
> over by the music?
> —Margaret Silf, *Inner Compass*

At the Religious Book Trade Show Exhibition in the spring of 2003, I met a heroic person. Father Gary Smith had written the book *Radical Compassion,* reflections on his work with the homeless and marginalized in Seattle. He had left this work and now ministered to an AIDS-stricken population in Uganda, Africa.

Over dinner, Father Smith told me about how the people in his area of Uganda could not even grow vegetables because the termites ate everything. *The termites ate everything:* any wood or straw on the houses, paper and glue in books, all greenery, everything. I lamely asked about insecticides (I am not a farmer's daughter for nothing), and he kindly told me that there was no money for such things and the problem was far too overwhelming and widespread.

Father Smith's eyes were liquid pools of pathos. They were eyes that had truly embraced the suffering of the world where there were no clear answers and theology falls apart. I don't think I have ever seen eyes like his, brimming over with sad Spirit, illumined by too much knowing, glowing with a crucified love. Christ's eyes must have looked like this, I thought.

In case I ever get inflated in my work—puffed up, as Scripture calls it—I only have to think of Father Smith. He is being crucified daily in a world filled with suffering that does not yield easily to answers. And yet I experienced him not as angry, judging or rigid; he exhibited compassion to me and to everyone that evening.

He was gently humorous, kind and respectful to Lyn Doucet who can order her life by calling the pest man, the plumber and the doctor. I am a person embarrassed by riches, of this there can be no doubt. He offered only acceptance even though, to quote one writer, I had been born on third base and often thought I had hit a triple. At this dinner, sipping my wine and munching my Italian salad, I was painfully aware that Father Smith looked after those who had never gotten their turn at bat.

I am clear that *my* call is to live out my life as a married woman with a son and, perhaps someday, grandchildren as well. My call is to live and love in the community where God has placed me. Yet I could surely live more by gospel values. I keep rolling back the same stone over and over: I encounter the resurrected Christ and let him have his way, and then I let him be buried in my life again. I don't fully enter into the resurrected life because I don't easily improve and release my selfishness. I fear suffering and lack far too much.

But there are certain long moments when my fear takes a back seat, the stone seems smaller, and I want live as Christ did. These are often moments when I am inspired by others. Their lives are like a sweet, faintly remembered music that penetrates my fear. These are the moments when I remember Father Gary Smith.

FOR REFLECTION AND JOURNALING

+ What is your response to this essay and to Father Smith's presence within it?

+ What gospel values are lacking in your life as you live your call?

CLOSING PRAYER

Say the Lord's Prayer.

Week Fourteen: Day Four

JUST PRESS IT

> This is what I am learning: To rest when weary. To stop eating when full. To walk away when saturated. I am learning to hear myself.
> —Paula D'Arcy, *Gift of the Red Bird*

When I was growing up I received much unconditional love from Blanche, the lady who helped care for us and clean the house while my parents worked. Blanche told me stories; she laughed often, sometimes becoming so tickled that she had to stop for a moment and regain her control. "Oh, Lyn?" She would almost shout, her voice jumping up to a quick crescendo ending with a rising question mark as she squeezed her wet eyes shut and shook her head over the latest story.

One day Blanche told me of how when she was growing up, very poor as many people around her were, her family would receive boxes of secondhand clothes from the church. She and her sisters would look hopefully through the clothes, trying things on. Blanch was thin, and often things would hang on her or billow around her small frame. Her mother would look up and say, "Well, just press it."

Just press it! Now Blanche was overcome by laughter, supporting her shaking body against the orange-tiled kitchen counter. *That was going to take care of everything; this dress was four sizes too big, but just press it! Oh...Lyn?* Wiping her eyes and glancing up at me while shaking her head, Blanche continued her work.

Blanche is gone now. I feel blessed that this memory of her came to me this morning as I lay in that grace-filled state of first waking. I think that the words *just press it* have something to say to our call.

The truth is that some of us go through life trying to live a call that does not fit. It may be a vocation that we inherited from another. It may be a ministry that those around us, perhaps in our church, have decided we are suited for. We stumble on, trying to fix it by small adjustments, to just press it and make it somehow fit. We haven't ever learned to listen to our own hearts because the voices of the community in which we are immersed are too strong. They drown everything else out. Many of us can't even stop when we are tired or drink when we are thirsty. We have to keep going and keep going. We must stop. We must listen within. We need to stop trying to make the wrong things fit.

FOR REFLECTION AND JOURNALING

+ Is your ministry or vocation the one you are truly called to do?

+ Are you staying there because it is comfortable, easy, what you have always done, or mainly because others want you there?

+ Is your suffering redemptive in the world, or is it unnecessary and not what God is asking at all?

+ You may find that you are truly where you are meant to be, living the vocation well-suited for your time and your talents. If so, rejoice! Rededicate. If not, it may be time to put up your pressing iron, and take out the real tools for change.

CLOSING PRAYER

Pray the Glory Be to the Father.

Week Fourteen: Day Five

HILL OF CROSSES

> For if we have been united with him in a death like his, we will certainly be united with him in a resurrection like his.
> —Romans 6:5

It was a gray and misty day when my niece Lara and I set out to go sightseeing. Lara and her husband, Milton, had become missionaries in Lithuania seven years before. Now I was visiting them and their two children in this struggling country, formerly a member of the Soviet block.

We traveled for many miles, seeing farmers with wagons, huge greenhouses, and high, stilted stork nests that were valued and protected as good luck symbols by the people. Mostly, we saw an uninhabited place. The empty land we traveled seemed as vast and featureless as the gray misty sky. Finally, we arrived at our destination and as Lara parked the car, I gasped.

This was the Hill of Crosses. Here, in the middle of nowhere, there were acres of crosses! There were huge and towering ones and tiny ones. There were crosses with prayers written upon them and crosses in memory of lost loved ones. We walked up hills and down trails, and we were surrounded by too many crosses to count, made of wood, glass, pottery, stone, crystal, plastic, even cloth and paper. There were thickets of crosses and every sort of arrangement of crosses. There seemed to be miles of crosses stretching into an endless distance.

No one knew exactly how it all started. Lara told me that the Russians had tried three times to eradicate the shrine, bulldozing it to the ground. But the crosses sprang up again, overnight, as though placed by invisible hands. These logos of faith would not be denied. The cross, that "symbol of suffering and shame," was stronger than political power, stronger than machines, stronger than oppression.

In the paschal mystery a suffering people found their truth and their hope for resurrection. And so do we, as we live daily in the call. Without the cross, our hopes and efforts are as nothing. Suffering stripped of meaning is only suffering, after all.

When I struggle to mend hostilities between two people from my church, and in doing so have that hostility directed at me, I embrace the cross. When I realize that I have gotten so involved with people that I *must* suffer with them over every loss, I embrace the cross. When the sacred concert for which I have practiced for weeks falls on its face because there are employee cuts at the local hospital and our guitarist has to stay there at work, I embrace a small cross. When I sit at my computer and words don't come and my neck hurts and I wonder why I ever wanted to be a spiritual writer, in my own way I embrace the cross. How would any of us go on without knowing there is a cross that enfolds our cross and transforms it with meaning, makes it larger, makes it sacred?

I blush to compare my small sufferings with those of an occupied and persecuted people such as the Lithuanians, but the fact that your cross and mine is smaller does not alter its shape. It is a cross, after all. And I gasp in wonder that all my doubts and failings have not been able to bulldoze its redemption away.

FOR REFLECTION AND JOURNALING
+ What is the cross for you?
+ How can it be redemptive in your life?
+ What necessary suffering is involved in your call, your life?

CLOSING PRAYER
On a hill far away,
Stood an old rugged cross,
The emblem of suffering and shame.
And I'll love that old cross,
Where the dearest and best,
For a world of lost sinners was slain.
—George Bennard, "The Old Rugged Cross"

Week Fourteen: Day Six

BE YOURSELF

> Protect your innocence by holding on to the truth; you are a child of God and deeply loved.
> —Henri Nouwen, *The Inner Voice of Love*

As we strive to be more like Jesus, more compassionate, more trusting and God-like, more courageous, we are also paradoxically called to be more ourselves. Our true selves. The call that we strive to live daily asks this of us: Be yourself.

As I write this, I smile because this was the advice given to young adolescent girls like me as we entered the mysterious, scary world of dating. "Just be yourself!" *Seventeen* magazine would trill confidently, this advice offered beside the picture of a flawlessly beautiful young woman with honeyed silky hair, dressed in the very latest magenta wool miniskirt and matching raw silk tailored blouse. Did they think that this advice solved our problems? I didn't have a self like the one pictured. I had no idea *who* "myself" was. I wanted to be a self that my date would approve of, so that he would ask me out again. I was not alone. A dear friend tells me that as she got ready for a party in her youth, she actually thought to herself, "Now I wonder who they would like me to be tonight?"

Getting to know this self, as we have seen, is a work of spirit and sweat. Christ knew this. He had to be who he was and live out his authentic call against tremendous resistance and pain. We must do the same, even if we are called to suffer also. For it is impossible to fully live our call while clinging to a counterfeit self.

We will also experience our truest joy as we use our authentic gifts. Hopefully we now know at least something about what these are. We have acquired tools that allow us to return again and again to the gold mine of our own authenticity. For the person that we are is fully sacred, truly the tool of God on this earth.

FOR REFLECTION AND JOURNALING

+ Write a paragraph about your true self as you live your call. What insecurities easily come to mind? Explore your gifts again.

CLOSING PRAYER

May the glory of the LORD endure forever;
    may the LORD rejoice in his works. Amen.
—from Psalm 104:31

Week Fourteen: Day Seven

LUMINOUS WITH GRACE

> Do you not see how this light shines even now in the
> hearts of the faithful—Do you not see how it is superior
> to the light of knowledge?
> —Saint Gregory Palamas

There is an ancient story from the Kabala saying that before the world was made, God was in one piece, and like unto a mirror. When the world was created, the mirror broke into a million fragments and scattered throughout the universe. Each created thing has a tiny bit of this mirror within them, giving to each a special luminosity, gift and power.

We are given gifts to enter this life, and we acquire gifts as we live—talents and attributes that are clearly meant to be used for good. In fact, we have gifts that are unique to each of us and are meant to fill a unique need in the world. We are designed to shine forth with the God within, the piece of the mirror that is ours alone. In cooperation with others our fragment joins with theirs, and the world's light grows stronger.

But we lose our way. We lose the truth of who we are and what we are called to do in this life. Our precious mirrors become silted over with the pressures and misconceptions of the society in which we live. We make decisions for the wrong reasons and lose the authenticity that is our birthright.

Saint Francis of Assisi had to suffer greatly to claim an authenticity and a life with God. He did not, overnight, become the saint who sang peaceful canticles to the sun and moon. He went through testing and trying along the way.

And yet, he seemed to have been sustained directly by the love of God. The light of God filled him as he wrestled with his own inner demons and the forces that sought to lead him away from his calling.

Unlike Francis, we forget that God has loved us unconditionally since our conception, and formed us in our mother's wombs. We were born with everything we need, surrounded by God's love and mercy. But the layers of life have caused us to forget this. We have grown up and rushed after false gods. A large part of this journey so far has led us into the healing we seek for the kingdom of God.

As we have seen, knowing the authentic self is a process, and it need not be rushed, in fact it must not be. Learn now to be a kind mother and father to the child of call within you. Be gentle with yourself, and do only the work you feel called to by the Spirit. Take a break when needed. Walk in the world of nature. Take a warm, sudsy bath, eat an ice cream cone. See an uplifting movie (*Seabiscuit,* anyone?). Remember that there is so much that is good in life. Choose it. It is a part of the call.

FOR REFLECTION AND JOURNALING
Look back over your journaling for the week and highlight major themes.

CLOSING PRAYER
Are any among you suffering? They should pray. Are any cheerful? They should sing songs of praise.
—James 5:13

Week Fifteen

Living and Loving with Freedom...Rejoice!

We are arriving at the end of a good journey.
It is time to rejoice and choose joy in every way.
Be surprised by all the goodness in your life!
Walk forth in gratitude for healing and call,
for God's Amazing Love!
And remember,
the journey never ends.
and that is Good News, indeed.

Week Fifteen: Day One

LESSONS FROM THE CANE FIELD

> Consider the lilies of the field, how they grow; they
> neither toil nor spin, yet I tell you, even Solomon in all
> his glory was not clothed like one of these.
> —Matthew 6:28–29

> There is such a power in the cosmic dance. Each time I
> resonate with this energy I sink into my soul and find
> a wide and wondrous connection with each part of
> my life.
> —Joyce Rupp, *The Cosmic Dance*

I first discovered my wonderful cane field simply by watching
my pets, Taffy and Charlie. They headed out the back gate
and into the field, and I decided to follow them. This is my
journal entry from that day:

> *It is a gorgeous day today in Maurice, Louisiana.*
> *The sky is clear blue and a distant yet warm sun*
> *shines down. The temperature is about sixty, and the*
> *air is wonderfully soft, with just a hint of crispness.*
> *I step out my back gate and into the sugar cane field,*
> *with Taffy, my sweet cocker-mix, coming to walk at*
> *my side. I have always known this field was here, but*
> *I never thought of walking here.*
>
> *I am instantly in a different world, as though pro-*
> *pelled onto an ancient island. There are only vast*
> *reaches of cane cut through with wide paths and*
> *roads. No people. No machines today. The cane is in*
> *many stages. Some of the field is cut, leaving only*
> *tawny stubble. Other portions of the cane have been*
> *blown down by a storm, looking beaten by a giant*

mixer. Portions of the field stand tall and their mellow colors fill me: ivory and rusty tan, taupe-green and true green, gold. The cane is bristling and yet still. Heavy with silence. Waiting and watching in being. Filled, for me, with the life of God.

This cane was planted by people, of course, but its essence seems untouched by humankind. It could have been growing here forever. It ripples with life. Birds start and dart up from its depths with a muffled whoosh. Rabbits hide on the edges. Hawks careen gustily overhead. This natural scene is complete and beautiful and healing; it is silent and present. Ah, the mystery of how it all comes to be and flourishes. Where does all this life come from after all, and why?

Now I feel the clean simplicity of nature filling me and healing me of chaos and busyness. The world is so much bigger than I am! My soul is saying, "This is it, this is life, uncomplicated by all your plans and little scenarios. This is real life." This is the world that neither toils nor worries, and I see its beauty at every turn, every moment.

For Reflection and Journaling

+ Describe experiences in nature that have expanded your soul. What lessons does nature teach us?
+ Can you live in the *now* at times, not worried about past or future?
+ What experiences of nature are close to where you live?

Closing Prayer

Write your own prayer of thanksgiving for the created world.

Week Fifteen: Day Two

BLESSED MEMORIES, HOW THEY LINGER...

> It should be know that God dwells secretly in all souls
> and is hidden in their substance, for otherwise they
> would not last.
> —Saint John of the Cross

> My child, I need you for Myself. I have purposes for
> your life beyond your comprehension. Open wide your
> heart to me...I will satisfy the deepest longing of your
> soul.
> —Frances J. Roberts, *Come Away My Beloved*

On a muddy day, I took a directee of mine, Jaycie, to walk
in the cane field. I just wanted to share the peace I found
there. She understood as we walked silently down the
muddy turn row. We didn't speak; we just walked among
the stalks and listened to the rustlings beneath them. The
indigo sky was etched with cloud messages; the chilly air
remembered things we had almost forgotten.

The cane brought back memories for her of childhood,
the days spent running around freely in and out of the lanes
and fields surrounding her home.

Jaycie had told me that once, years ago, she had seen a
tiny, exquisite flower in Girard Park, and she bent to pick
it. As she leaned forward, she suddenly knew that she, too,
was a part of God's creation, too, a welcomed part. She left
the flower, but this experience was a part of her turning
toward reconciliation.

Life for Jaycie was filled with woundings, and leavings
and broken dreams. Ah...but hidden in all this was her purpose. Looking at that tiny flower and walking in the cane
field opened wide her heart. She understood things that she

had not before: that the love that created perfection in a tiny flower was the love that ordered her destiny. It had always been with her, dancing with her in fields of long ago, holding her gently all these years and calling her home.

FOR REFLECTION AND JOURNALING

+ Go out and see nature today. Look at the sky, the trees, the birds. Breathe the air deeply and notice the rays of sunlight and the clouds. The secret to life is to be here now. This is the gift we are given. What are the sometimes unrecognized gifts that the natural world has brought to your life?

CLOSING PRAYER

Make a joyful noise to the LORD, all the earth.
    Worship the LORD with gladness;
    come into his presence with singing.
Know that the LORD is God.
    It is he that made us, and we are his;
    we are his people, and the sheep of his pasture.
Enter his gates with thanksgiving,
    and his courts with praise.
    Give thanks to him, bless his name.
For the LORD is good;
    his steadfast love endures for ever,
    and his faithfulness to all generations.
—Psalm 100

Week Fifteen: Day Three

DESTRUCTION?

After many days of walking in the cane field, I saw that black smoke was rising from it and billowing to the sky. The after-harvest burning of the fields was taking place. I was glad that I had walked as much as I had, and taken in the beauty of the place before it was turned to charred ashes. I stood and watched the devastation of the flames; I was not happy.

At another time, I might not have noticed, but I had been tramping the cane field for weeks, happily walking with my dogs or my friends. In the field I saw a life's land-scape, with turns and twists and hidden meanings. I hoped the tiny animals would have a place to go; surely they would run into the woods nearby. Now the fields would be charred black instead of glowing with tawny golden life. Ah, life is change. Life is always changing.

FOR REFLECTION AND JOURNALING

+ What has changed now in your life?
+ How does nature reflect both destructive and healing changes?

CLOSING PRAYER

I wonder if what seems to be all darkness, God,
Hides a wondrous life,
The way dark stormy clouds bring rain,
Watering the parched landscape and filling the reservoirs of the earth. Amen.

Week Fifteen: Day Four

THE GREENING IS ALWAYS THERE...

> My soul, where does this breathing arise?
> How does the beating heart exist?
> Bird of the soul, speak in your own words,
> and I will understand.
> —Jelaluddin Rumi, *Love is a Stranger*

Grace breaks in where we least anticipate it.
—Phillip Bennett, *Let Yourself Be Loved*

This morning I walked out to my office in back of my home and near the cane field. The sun is shining today. In the field I notice now that greening is coming; new shoots are appearing on all the stalks. A resurrection is occurring.

A bright cardinal rests among the stalks, his coat a crimson relief against the burned stalks. The animals come slowly back, the killdeers stagger around on their straight legs, coveys of quail sploosh up! Up! White-marked brown rabbits hop out of the woods and look around, sniffing, nibbling the air. Life renews itself. It goes on; nature copes as we must when we face changes. Soon the rain will wash all the blackness away.

FOR REFLECTION AND JOURNALING

+ How does this all come to be? As Annie Dillard says, "Is this where we live? With the air so light and free?" How does my beating heart exist? And how can we not respond with love and giving to a world so heartbreakingly beautiful? How can we not sing alleluia to a God who makes all things new?
+ How could nature nourish you today?
+ Write a poem about the natural world.

CLOSING PRAYER

Creating God, you make all things new.
Resurrection is your name.
In misty rain and egg-yolk sun, you give us life.
Your grace is connecting us to all that lives.
Where we have only seen destruction,
Your abundant life bursts forth again and again. Amen.

Week Fifteen: Day Five

DEEPLY TOUCHED BY GIFT

> This is it. My life. How I respond, whether or not I am
> ready to open doors to larger places, will determine
> what I realize and what my life will be.
> —Paula D'Arcy, *Seeking with All My Heart*

My new friends Susan, Kathleen and I recently visited a
wild flower refuge on an early spring day. The enchanted
place we visited had been designed and lived in by Caroline
Dorman, a Louisiana naturalist who lived earlier in the
century. A hardy and liberated woman, she had left the
mark of her call in beauty both rugged and fragile. Her rus-
tic home spoke volumes of where her treasure lay. The
world of growing things had received her full attention and
care, as every native plant she could lay hands on (some
endangered) had been transported to her corner of the
earth, where they now flourished.

It was a blessed day for the three of us, as everything
was blooming, displaying soft pinks and purples, with
mosses dipping over green water like a Monet painting and
wild azaleas displaying oranges and yellows we had never
seen before.

As we drove home filled with the sweet ache of beauty,
a fine mist began to coat our windshield while the sun still
shone.

"Look out for rainbows," I said. "The conditions are just
right."

We rounded a bend, and suddenly there was not one
rainbow but two. This double rainbow was so enormous
that we seemed to be traveling *in* it. I was shot through
with wonder and felt as though I had entered a different

dimension. The quality of light, the prayerful presence of my friends, the brilliant color that saturated the air, all transported me to a mysterious and sacred place.

"Perhaps this is what heaven is like," I thought. When we stopped for supper, we shared the wonder and thankfulness each of us felt. We were new friends, all participating in a year-long prayer journey together. Now in an ever-deepening way, we spoke of sign and symbol, of grace and mystery. We felt chosen and loved.

Ah, it's the *kingdom* of heaven, now I see. Surprised by joy, we had the grace of knowing, if only for a moment, that everything was gift.

FOR REFLECTION AND JOURNALING

+ Can you remember a similar time in your life?
+ When are you able to rejoice? When are you surprised by joy?
+ What are important symbols to you?

CLOSING PRAYER

God, your people, centuries ago,
stood shaken at the thunder in the sky.
You gave them a rainbow, arched across the heavens.
Built of colors, still it comes, it goes.
Build now a rainbow
across my trembling heart,
so that I can feel it,
so that I can be it.
so I can rejoice again in you. Amen.

Week Fifteen: Day Six

ONE CARDINAL

> And for all this, nature is never spent;
>> There lives the dearest freshness deep down things;
> And though the last lights off the black West went
>> Oh, morning, at the brown brink eastward springs—
> Because the Holy Ghost over the bent
>> World broods with a warm breast and with ah!
> bright wings.
> —Gerald Manley Hopkins, "God's Grandeur"

It is a cool and beautiful morning, and I am tugging on my jeans. My chattering mind is rapidly planning my day.

Then I look out my bedroom window, and a brilliant male cardinal alights against the thicket of Chinese tallow trees just outside. He sits there for many moments amidst the fallen-leaf grays and muted greens of the branches, shining in the filtered sunlight. He pauses in all his beauty, pulsing with scarlet life.

A thought comes to me, "This ought to be enough. Seeing this should be enough."

I often write about cardinals. We have many; they flutter in flocks; they swoop around my home in chummy groups enjoying the bounty of Chinese tallow berries. I discovered, when I journeyed to certain other states, that they are rare. When one appears, people truly notice and are gratified by the presence.

Can I be happy with just one? I am scandalized by my own seeking and grasping: more stuff, more comfort, more safety and more experiences. I forget that I already have all I need. I can be like a starving woman at a banquet; I am so busy finding the right chair to sit in and the right people to sit by that I miss the feast—until a ruddy flame of grace enters and jerks me back to where all goodness lies.

FOR REFLECTION AND JOURNALING

+ As you reach toward the end of this prayer journey, what have been its major gifts in your life?
+ How can you bring those gifts into your daily life?
+ How could you express your gifts of healing? In a ritual? A painting? A story or poem?
+ Write a poem of gratitude.

CLOSING PRAYER

Wake me up, Lord. Let me see *today,* that creation of hovering Spirit,
Gift of bright wings.
Wake me up to the bounty, the beauty that surrounds me now.
Open my eyes. Help me to *really* see,
For sometimes I just say that I do. Amen.

Week Fifteen: Day Seven

LED BY THE SPIRIT: FULLY AT HOME

In his book, *Awakenings,* Thomas Keating speaks of Jesus being led to Nazareth by the Spirit. Keating says, "He did not go there of his own initiative. He was following a movement of Spirit within him with whom he was totally identified. God is infinite concern for every living thing. That is the source of every true mission or ministry in the church. It is not our work. It is a movement of love in the Trinity."[12] Jesus was living in the kingdom of God.

We live in the kingdom in our bodies, doing our everyday tasks. In thinking about this, I ponder that I try to be compassionate to myself as my body ages. I sometimes muse about the truth of the statement, "We are spiritual beings having a human experience." I wonder what it would be like to throw off the body and—fly! And I am sure I will think of this much more as the years go by. And I think also about the exiled feelings I sometimes have, feelings that are expressed in old spirituals with words like, *this world is not my home*. There is a part of all of us that perhaps longs for the heavenly home that we hope for.

And yet—and yet, God made us with bodies and put us here, not so that we would spend our time seeking to escape from the experience. God put us here to live, to love, to celebrate, to suffer, to *be*.

And so I pray: *God, for today, let me be here now. Let me dance in the movement of love that is the Trinity. Let me be called by Spirit at your initiative. For you are infinite concern for every living thing. And you have brought me home to your kingdom.*

I long to be like Saint Francis of Assisi, who experienced the kingdom in a unique way as he turned away from all that had been home to him. As he rejected riches and comfort, he found his home in Christ alone. He was immersed in the love and goodness that he saw in all things.

So as we close our journey together, I ask you to consider being fully here and fully home in Jesus, immersed in love and the good things of this earth. You have done many things during our weeks together, and I hope you are stronger in spirit and mind. I hope that you know that God who has begun a good work in you will see it to the finish. I pray you will be kind and gentle to yourself and others. The world does not need more competition, more getting, more pushing, more noise. The world needs the silence of love that I pray has been birthed within your heart.

I am in the *kingdom of God* when:

- My mind is still and peaceful.
- I see things around me clearly; I see and appreciate those people I encounter.
- I am not worried. I am not planning. I am being.
- I treat those I meet with compassion, and I embrace myself with the same compassion.
- I embrace a suffering world without turning away or becoming cynical.
- I am not in a hurry to be somewhere else or do something else.
- I tune in to my senses: I enjoy my lunch, the song of a bird, or a baby in the park.
- I am grateful for what I have in my life. I am not clutching for more.
- I know that *this* is the kingdom of heaven.
- I can love you without clinging to you.

FOR REFLECTION AND JOURNALING
Take some time to review your prayer journal for the week. You may want to use a highlighter to underline themes and different ideas that are coming into awareness. Spend some time resting in God in the *now*.

CLOSING PRAYER
You may want to pray the Abba prayer on pages 102–103.

EPILOGUE

What a difference a day can make.
After weeks of cold rain, I see signs of spring!
Clumps of clover, daffodils pushing up,
scented bloom on the sweet tea olive...
It amazes me how quickly life comes forth.
And I pray life has burst forth in you,
with all beauty and grace.

My friends, I bid you a sort of goodbye.
You probably won't live with my words every day, any more!
And that is good, because there are so many words to discover,
and worlds of ideas and plans in Christ's kingdom of love.

Laugh, be silly, go barefoot, play.
Look at the daffodils,
smell all the roses.
You have earned it. Rejoice!
And go forth with courage, for I trust you continue to be
healed and called
in many, many ways...every day!
All this you will discover as life unfolds.

Part Two: Group Workshop

THE HEALING GROUP: AN OVERVIEW

Why form a group?

Years ago when I was a young mother, I invited three other couples to join my husband and me in forming a spiritual group. I knew I wanted more intimacy than church provided; I was seeking more meaning in my spiritual life.

The bad news was that we knew nothing at that time about forming a group or engaging in a group process. The good news was that the group worked despite our ignorance and bumbling, propelled along by the Spirit and the basic good will that we shared.

Chris and Ricky, Dale and Ginger, Yvette and Barry, Lyn and Dee, the six of us agreed to meet monthly in each other's homes to read Scripture, discuss psychology or a book of choice or to examine our lives in general. We were all young parents, struggling with family and career, and, breaking all the rules of group process, we tried to solve each others' problems and change one another. I was the absolute worst participant because for some reason I thought I was supposed to give everyone advice, which I did while (for a long time) studiously avoiding my own inner work.

Perhaps I gave advice because I was a teacher and was too comfortable with that persona, or perhaps it was because I come from a long line of fiercely independent people who give advice well, rather than take it! However, my heart was in the right place and I learned much. We persisted in our efforts and the group lasted in an organized way for about three years until we amicably agreed to stop meeting.

But here is the miracle: to this day we are all close, and refer to ourselves as "the group." This is mystery and wonder, that our bond has survived arguments and misunderstandings, the divorce of one of our couples, and the pain and withdrawal of various members at various times. Despite all of this, the love remains. We rarely leave one another's presence without saying, "I love you," and hearing, "I love you, too." We are now supporting each other through the weddings of children and the death of parents.

We are truly available and present for one another. It seems that once masks have been lowered and true intimacy achieved, true love flows. Perhaps this is especially true when the group meets under the guidance of Christ and seeks (however unskillfully) God's will for each person.

Once the six of us spontaneously took a walk along the Vermilion River, a walk that lasted for hours and culminated at another friend's camp with toasts of cold white wine. We laughed the whole trip. One group member, Ginger, said years after this adventure, "That was one of the best days of my life." Our group process taught us to laugh freely together, to celebrate life where we are, as we are. We are bedrock safe with each other. We can enjoy life with one another without fear, masks or posturing. Because of this, we have grown in courage and in our faith. It is a place for us to understand and live this reality. At its best it is a compassionate container for our sorrow and a reflective container for insight and growth. We become more fully converted to Christ as we understand ourselves and others as well as our roles in Christ's kingdom of love. At its best, the healing group brings us home to God's unconditional love. As we grow and heal we are called to service in the Body of Christ.

As I look back, I see that by abundant grace, we did do

many things right. We learned that only unconditional love changes another. Yet we challenged one another. Not only did we form intimacy, we grew spiritually. We had to. The group forced us to look inside and finally even I had to face my pain and decide what to do about it. I begin to embrace a call from God that was authentic, even though difficult. Today I think that I would not be a spiritual director and author if I had not begun to wrestle with God, and with my false sense of self, in this group.

Being with them allowed me to articulate ideas that were hard to put into words. My friends listened and encouraged me, seeing in me what I couldn't see in myself. Most importantly, we listened to God's voice together in community, and we all grew in our Christian walk. There was a power for growth within the group that wasn't present in a therapy session or a one-on-one conversation, though these are good things indeed. It was the power of Christ gathered to strengthen all present. A conversion of our hearts took place, as we began to be critical of the voice of cultural consciousness and to tune in to God's voice within us. This led us all to service in the larger community.

Why is there a need for healing groups?
The psychologist John Bradshaw states that the religion of the United States is optimism and denial. He says we like for people to be "happy and fine," and do not encourage them to communicate with us if they are not. I would add that another dimension of our consensual spirituality is a rugged self-determinism and individualism. We were a country in which men (and I use that term on purpose) controlled their own destinies, conquered through their own efforts, wrested a living alone with gritted teeth—and by golly, it worked!

However, the shadow side of this individualistic and self-determined style has raised its ugly head and threatens us in many ways. Psychological depression is rampant in our country, and suicide claims more teens than accidents do. A cursory glance at the newspaper reveals epidemics of domestic and child abuse. In my spiritual direction practice I encounter person after person who is deeply lonely. We really are not happy and fine.

In addition to rugged individualism, we share a history of community-building as well. Strong communities and churches have defined our country. However, the mobility of our society, its changing institutions and the obvious breakdown of both extended and nuclear family...all these factors have left us confused and searching for new sources of support.

For Christians, community-building is a return to our ancient roots. Jesus lived and worked in community, gathering around him friends with whom to pray, work and break bread. His life reflected the perfect balance of solitary prayer and time spent in sharing and service with others. Saint Paul continued this tradition. The first Christian churches were, in fact, small communities that met in homes. These early Christians shared Eucharist and bore one another's burdens.

In theory, of course, our churches are still communities with shared beliefs and common goals. Many churches promote friendship and even intimacy among their members. This is difficult as the priest shortage deepens and parishes grow larger. In churches with strong liturgical demands, intimacy may not be as easy to achieve. The Sunday school classes of protestant denominations sometimes serve well, but we don't have a direct parallel to this in other faith walks.

The small church movement has been formed to solve

some of these problems. "Come, Lord Jesus," groups and prayer circles of many types have sprung up. Bible study is becoming popular in many of our parishes. It is very helpful to share insight about the Bible in supporting groups.

One cannot speak of healing groups without mentioning twelve step/addiction programs such as A.A. The stunning success of these meetings has led author Scott Peck to deem them, "the most important contribution of western spirituality." This statement certainly gives us pause. We are led to ask, "What have people found in these groups?" An interview of participants in these programs gives us these answers: Unconditional acceptance. Safety and trust. Intimacy. Accountability. Healing. A container for doubts, fears and sufferings. A place to finally tell the truth. A place to heal brokenness. Companionship in the struggle. Hope in God.

These are surely worthy goals for any small group. Not all groups succeed in their efforts. The shadow side of group dynamics occurs when groups become clannish or suspicious of those outside the circle. Problems occur when one person seizes too much power, imposes his or her ideas or seeks to influence others unduly. Membership in a group should never interfere with another's freedom.

There is much suffering in our world. Mother Teresa says it poignantly, "You in the West suffer psychologically." As Christians we know that both suffering and joy, indeed the paschal mystery itself, comes to all. The healing group offers a place to make sense of suffering. Suffering has meaning and value when it becomes transformative, when it is linked to the suffering of Christ in the context of our own lives. The healing group offers a place where we encounter the mystery of suffering in a constructive way.

I meet monthly with a group of women who are Theresians, which is an international organization taking as its patron Thérèse, the Little Flower of Lisieux. There are eleven of us, and the group has met for three years. During this time we have undergone many changes, and members have come and gone. Although I knew most of the people in the group before we started, we have deepened our relationships and have achieved a new level of intimacy. We have gone through a honeymoon period and a chaotic time when we wondered fearfully whether the group would survive. We have survived, and we continue to be strengthened.

We pray for one another's vocation, whether in the home, the marketplace or the larger church community. We celebrate the sacredness in one another. Because of my experience in my first group (and formal education in group process, also) I bring a different dynamic to this new group. I listen, I am calmer. I know that the growth of each member and of our small community is held in God's hands.

I am also meeting with a brand new group of writers. We are as unformed as an amoeba. We are casting around to find our purpose. We may or may not make it as a long-term group, yet we have already forged friendships through our common bond. The process of forming group is exciting indeed.

My experiences of group process have been richly rewarding and life-giving. I am honored to share information about this process with many others. I know that a group can lead us to the heart of conversion. We more and more put aside our foolish distractions and seek the Lord. As we encourage more and more group formation in our parishes and communities, various tools will be needed for the process. I hope this book can be important resource for many, helping to form and maintain conversion/healing/sharing groups of all kinds.

THE ORGANIZATIONAL MEETING

This meeting will be held before each individual's prayer with the book begins, but after publicity has been done, and group members have been contacted by phone or E-mail as to the initial meeting day and time. Ask members to obtain books beforehand, or have books available at the meeting. Arrange a simple altar and have a candle placed, ready to light. Encourage everyone to dress comfortably.

If at all possible, meet in someone's home. However, initial meetings can also be held in churches or other public areas, even at bookstores.

Schedule at least ninety minutes for this meeting. Two hours is optimum, for example, from 6:30 until 8:30 in the evening. It is important that meetings always start and end on time.

Leadership for meetings can rotate. One member agrees to be the leader for the initial, organizational meeting.

A Word about Group Prayer and Ritual

We live in a fast paced and hyperactive world. Group process such as this involves an invitation to slow down. This may take some getting used to, but don't be afraid of silence. Don't be afraid of pauses in activity and speech. It is in the pauses that Spirit can do good work in our hearts.

The prayers and rituals provided here must be done slowly and with reverence or they will have little value. Take your time. Be fully present. Savor your time together.

Agenda for the Organizational Meeting

Gather the group in a circle and make introductions. Allow time for some conversation.

The leader lights a candle and says the opening prayer: "Come, Holy Spirit, and enliven us this day. As we embark on a new adventure and embrace a Healing Walk, come close to us and guide us. We trust in your goodness. You fill our hearts with love and hope. Amen."

Invite discussion or questions after going over the following rules for group process:

- Group members will have an innate sense about what is shared by members that must be kept confidential. This is a sacred trust. Group members must not share confidential material even with their spouses. (However, there are many aspects of group dynamics that they can share freely.)
- Every person in the group is an equal. Treat one another with kindness and respect. Ideally, leadership will circulate among the members, each taking a meeting as needed.
- Listening is the most important job of a group member. This involves turning away from our own inner dialogue and really tuning in to the person speaking.
- Allow brief silence after the person speaking finishes. No interrupting or rapid responses. (Some authors call this "cross-talking." Allow time to respond, not react.)
- Do not give advice. Remember, God is the healer.
- Allow each person time to speak. While no one should be pressured to speak, part of being a good group member is to share what one is thinking and feeling.
- Keep comments brief enough so that time permits each person to share. Don't get lost in unimportant details. It is the inner journey that is important.
- Share your own experience from your heart. For each person in the group this should be a heart, not a head, journey.
- Groups of this type are different from discussion groups where knowledge is the most important thing.
- Accept differences in beliefs and practices.
- Be committed to meeting with the group.

Opening Prayer Ritual

Invite the group to be seated and to center themselves—relax and release the pressures of the day. Invite them to tune in to their breathing, breathing gently in and out, focusing on being fully present in the circle. Soft instrumental music is a nice addition to this service. You may want to have a green plant, a wine cup or some grapes on the altar.

Prayer

Leader: God, we believe that you have brought us together this day for a purpose. Fill us with your love and your goodness. Help us to be gentle, kind and compassionate with one another. Let us bear one another's burdens. Open our ears and our eyes, and let us be light for one another. May we bear fruit in your kingdom. Amen.

Response: God's faithful love lasts forever.

Leader: Give thanks to God for he is good, his faithful love endures forever. God redeems us, bringing us home from foreign lands.

Response: God's faithful love lasts forever.

Leader: We have wandered in the desert; we were hungry and thirsty. Our life's forces burned low. We cried out to you and you rescued us and shattered the chains that held us bound.

Response: God's faithful love lasts forever.

Leader: We will sow new fields and plant new vines; a good harvest is in our future. You bless us and our numbers increase. You cover us with blessings.

Response: God's faithful love lasts forever.

Observe a short period of silence.

Gospel reading

John 15:1–5

Leader: And Jesus said, "I am the true vine, and my

Father is the vine-grower. He removes every branch in me that bears no fruit. Every branch that bears fruit he prunes to make it bear more fruit. You have already been cleansed by the word that I have spoken to you. Abide in me as I abide in you. Just as the branch cannot bear fruit by itself unless it abides in the vine, neither can you unless you abide in me." The Word of the Lord.

Response: Thanks be to God.

Play quiet music for five minutes while each person silently meditates on the prayer and the gospel reading.

(Optional: If desired, there can be brief sharing concerning the readings.)

Holding hands, close prayer ritual with the Lord's Prayer.

Activity
Getting Acquainted

Each person repeats his or her name, and tells a little about his or her life situation (working, married or not, children, member of church and so on, or whatever seems appropriate). What is each hoping to gain from the group? Have there been other group experiences? Were they positive, negative? Does the member have any suggestions for how the group should proceed?

Activity
Preparing for Individual Prayer

The leader goes over the upcoming week's material in the book, emphasizing areas of particular interest to the group. Invite discussion or questions.

Business Matters

Set next meeting date and time.

Social time and refreshments

Break for coffee, socializing if desired and/or if there is time. You may wish to establish a schedule for group members to bring snacks or refreshments.

Closing Prayer

Gather the group for final prayer.

Leader: Lord, it is our hope that we will become more firmly grafted to the vine that is you. We leave this evening with hope and joy. Thank you for new friends and old. Thank you for the life of Spirit in this world. Amen.

Depart

Week One

LOOKING AHEAD: BEGINNING A PRAYER JOURNEY

Gathering

Gather the group near the altar area. Have everyone be seated; light the candle.

Spend five minutes relaxing and breathing in silence.

Opening Prayer

Leader: God, we have hearts filled with hope this evening. We want to become strong in all our broken places. We want to develop our gifts and lay them upon your altar. Be with us now as we begin. We know you love us. We love you, too. Strengthen us in this love. Amen.

Observe silence for three minutes or so.

Discussion

Go around the circle and reintroduce yourselves. There may be new members present for the first time. Tell a little about yourselves.

Activity
Partner Work

Each person will pair with a partner. It is best if your partner is someone you don't know very well. Separate into partner pairs to share journal work and discuss how your individual prayer is going. Cover these areas: Spaciousness, being called, awareness and openness, and so on.

When the group comes back together, discuss in general both the successes and difficulties in establishing and maintaining prayer. The leader may want to ask members what is working best for each.

Break

Break for refreshments and conversation

Looking Ahead

When group regathers, discuss next week's prayer chapters and the time and place for meeting.

Optional Activity
Petitionary Prayer

Each member raises his or her petitions and the group response is: *Hear our prayer, O Lord.*

Closing Prayer

Leader: As we go to our homes, we keep one another close, close in our heart.

Response: Keep us close, O Lord.

Leader: Let us pray for one another as we journey on, knowing we are not alone.

Response: Keep us close, O Lord.

Leader: Keep each member of our group safe and immersed in your love.

Response: Keep us close, O Lord.

Leader: We pray for the families represented here, the

communities and churches too.

Response: Keep us close, O Lord.

Leader: And trusting in your love for us, we now offer each other a sign of peace.

Exchange the sign of peace.

Week Two

LOOKING WITHIN: A SPIRITUAL CHECKUP

(Note: As meetings progress and tender places in the heart are probed, tears may flow. Don't be afraid of tears! This is the way our hearts are healed. Don't feel that if someone cries you must do something about it. Just be present in respectful silence. However, if needed, the group may certainly comfort a grieving member as they deem appropriate.)

Gathering

Gather the group, in a circle if possible, near a simple altar area. When the group is seated, light a candle.

Take some moments of silence to center the group. The leader may want to instruct everyone to release the stresses of the day, and center in God's silent presence (allow at least five minutes).

Opening Prayer

Leader: Lord, you are searching our hearts and finding our strong and broken places.

Response: O Lord, you search us and you know us.

Leader: We look at our spiritual lives and see how you are present with us.

Response: O Lord, you search us and you know us.

Leader: Forgive us, God, for the times we have turned away from your love.

Response: O Lord, you search us and you know us.

Leader: Welcome the love within us and saturate it with your own love.

Response: O Lord, you search us and you know us.

Leader: God, as we place our spiritual lives in your care, help us to know how you are working within us, even at this moment, even at every single moment of our lives. Amen.

Discuss

The leader asks these questions:

How is everyone tonight? How has your week been? Has there been time to pray?

As you went through the spiritual checkup, what areas of your spiritual life were calling out for improvement?

What areas seem strong and healthy?

(Note: Set a time limit for this discussion, but do not worry if you cannot finish. This is not important. It is important to give those members who need attention the support of the group. As leader, be careful not to monopolize the conversation.)

Break

Break for refreshments and conversation (allow about fifteen minutes).

Looking Ahead

The leader asks: What have we discovered this evening?

As leader, direct the members' attention to next week's prayer chapters in the book. Encourage general discussion on how the group feels about the subject that is coming up.

Make plans for the next meeting, time and place. Ask the members to bring next time an item that is used in their work. (An engineer might bring a slide rule, a teacher her grade book, and so on.)

Closing Prayer

The group joins hands and prays the Lord's Prayer. The meeting ends with a sign of peace.

Week Three

LOOKING ABOUT: FINDING MY LIFE NOW

Gathering

The altar holds just a candle tonight. As the members gather, ask them to place their work items on the altar. Spend some minutes getting centered in silence.

Opening Prayer

Leader: Our work and our families, our churches, God, are gifts, and everything we have is gift from you.

Response: You will show us the path of life.

Leader: Let us never take these gifts for granted. May our hearts be lifted in gratitude.

Response: You will show us the path of life.

Leader: Let us see also, Lord, how you call us to change and to growth. Let us be watchful, yet gentle with ourselves.

Response: You will show us the path of life.

Leader: O Lord, as we speak from our hearts, be near us. Keep us centered always in you.

Response: You will show us the path of life. Amen.

Discussion

How does your work affect your spiritual life? Are overwork and stress an issue for you? What are the positive things you encounter in your work life? What did you write in your journal about your worshipping community? What relationships are most important to you? Which relationships are changing? What changes is God urging you toward, if any, at this time?

Break

Break for conversation and refreshments.

Looking Ahead

Regroup and discuss the time and place for the next meeting. Discuss how the meetings are going. The leader presents the following questions and invites comment:

- Has everyone had time to express him or herself at the last two meetings?
- Is this meeting format working for the group? Are any adjustments needed?
- Is the amount of prayer assigned working for the members?
- Is any group member uncomfortable with any part of the process?
- Is there any part of the meeting that needs expansion, that is, more time? Less time?

Everyone should look ahead in the books to preview the next material to be covered. The leader reminds members to bring their lifelines to the meeting. The leader will also need to have copies of: "I Will Never Forget You, My People" (from Isaiah 49) by Carey Landry for the next meeting. This song is in most hymnbooks.

Closing Prayer

Petitionary prayer around the circle is optional. Share final thoughts. What have we learned this evening?

Hold hands, recite the Lord's Prayer and close with a sign of peace.

Week Four

LOOKING BACK: THE LIFELINE

Gathering

The group gathers around the altar area and begins the meeting by holding hands and saying the Lord's Prayer.

The leader should ask how everyone is feeling. In general, has God felt close or far away this week? How well is prayer proceeding? The leader then explains the partner activity.

Activity

Partners

Each person partners with another at random. It is helpful to choose someone who you don't know well. Separate into pairs and discuss the lifeline of each partner. This will take at least thirty minutes if it is done well. Be patient and caring with one another. Remember to share only to the level that is comfortable for each.

Break

Break for refreshments and conversation.

Discussion

When the group gathers, the leader asks them each to share when God has been most present in their lives. A person may want to give more than one example.

The leader then asks if anyone wants to share a time of desolation, when God felt far away. (Note: Some members will ponder things in their hearts silently. This is fine.)

Looking Ahead

Discuss plans for next meeting, and turn to the pages of the book to preview that section if desired. Remind members to bring their prayer journals to the next meeting.

Ritual

Everyone stands near the altar holding his or her own lifeline. Remain in silence for a few minutes. Play or sing a song, such as "I Will Never Forget You, My People," by Carey Landry, while, taking turns, each person places his or her lifeline on the altar.

When the song is finished, remain in silence for some minutes, looking toward the altar area and praying silently. If desired, have the group hold hands.

Leader: O, Lord of consolation, you grace our life path. You have been with us, even when we didn't see your face. You have been with us. Be with us still as we travel on. Lead us beside the still waters of your love. For you are our shepherd, and we shall want for nothing. Amen.

(The group now extends blessing hands over the altar.)

Response: Dear Lord, you have been traveling with us all our lives. Help us to know and recognize your presence. Make us mindful of your love for us as we journey on. Bless our lives as represented by these lifelines. Amen.

Closing Prayer

Close with a sign of peace.

Week Five

GROUNDED IN LOVE: THE PROMISES OF JOHN 15

(Note to the leader: I have supplied a lot of material for this meeting, including a guided meditation. Read over all the material and decide what you would like to use. It is suggested that two hours be dedicated to this meeting.)

Gathering

The group gathers around a simple altar area. Decorate the altar with a green plant (ivy is nice), icons, a Bible and some candles. Play quiet instrumental music, if desired. The Vince Abrosetti song "I Am the Vine" from the recording *Come All Who Labor* could be used any time during the meeting.

Opening Prayer

Leader: Lord, we are traveling in a prayer journey with you and together. Lift our hearts with love and gratitude. You have given all to us. We celebrate your goodness. Shine a light into each corner of our hearts and bring us healing.

Response: Amen.

Ritual

Invite the group to center themselves, relax and release the pressures of the day. Invite them to tune in to their breathing, breathing gently in and out, focusing on being fully present in the circle.

Leader: I am the true vine and my Father is the vine-dresser.

Response: Remain in me.

Leader: Every branch in me that bears no fruit, he cuts away; and every branch that does bear fruit, he prunes to make it bear even more.

Response: Remain in me.

Leader: As a branch cannot bear fruit all by itself, unless it remains part of the vine, neither can you be fruitful, unless you remain in me. I am the vine, you are the branches.

Response: Remain in me.

Leader: Whoever remains in me, and I remain in that one, bears fruit aplenty. For, cut off from me, you can do nothing, like the branch that is thrown away and withers.

Response: Remain in me.

Leader: If you remain in me and I in you, you may ask for whatever you wish, and you will get it.

Response: Remain in me.

Leader: It is the glory of the Father that you bear much fruit. You are my friends if you do what I command. I no longer call you servants, because a servant does not know the master's business. I call you friends because I have made known to you all that I have learned from my Father.

Response: Remain in me.

Leader: You did not choose me. I chose you! I commissioned you to go out and bear much fruit. Remember, love one another.

Response: Remain in me.

Leader: Lord, let us show respect and love for one another as we continue our journey together. Open our hearts to one another.

Response: Amen.

Discussion

(Note for the leader: This may be a time that people want to preach to or fix others. Gently remind each to talk of his or her own experiences. This will be difficult for some people because they want to speak what is right. It is hard for them to assimilate that this journey is not about right and wrong.)

The leader begins the discussion for the week by asking group members to turn to their journaling and asking: As you reread the John 15 text, are you at all surprised that Jesus calls us all *friends?* What would a friendship with God be like? Is there anything else anyone would like to share concerning ups and downs during their week? When do you feel most grafted to Jesus, the vine? When do you feel diminished, not flourishing in him?

Break

Break for coffee and socializing if desired and if there is time.

Looking Ahead

Regather in the circle for final thoughts. Some groups like to check in with other members by phone before the next meeting. Some groups have prayer partners and share coffee and thoughts between group meetings. This is optional. Discuss the logistics of the next meeting. Remind the members to bring their books and prayer journals

Closing Prayer

Leader: Lord, support us in our prayer time with you this week. We long to grow closer to you and heal the loneliness we often feel. Keep us grafted to the vine. Help us love one another and keep your commandments Walk with us and keep us in your peace until we meet again. Amen.

Offer one another a sign of peace.

Additional Material

Below is a guided meditation that may be used at the group meeting in place of the prayer ritual or at another time. In my retreat work, I have found guided meditations very effective. Many people tell me that this is a vivid experience of prayer for them.

Vineyard Meditation

(Note: Have someone read this aloud to those meditating. Read slowly, with pauses. Play soft background music. You can also record this, and play it back as needed.)

Leader: Close your eyes and center your breathing. Breathe slowly from your center, in through your nose and out through your mouth. Release your tension. You may have many thoughts that run through your mind. Just observe them. Don't try to stop them; don't hold on to them. Observe them like clouds floating across the sky. (Allow for a short pause, here.)

Imagine yourself in a beautiful vineyard. The vines are

tilled and healthy, loaded with fruit. The leaves are glossy and green. As you walk slowly down the rows, you see grapes of many colors: red and purple, blue and yellow, green and white. These grapes are ripe and bursting with juice, glistening with dewdrops. How beautiful the vineyard is!

The air is cool, and the sun is warm upon your face. A gentle breeze blows. The sky is blue. Surrounding the vineyard are beds of beautiful flowers. The beds are carefully tended, and the flowers are of many types and colors: roses, daisies, pansies, lilies, tiny wild flowers and other flowers, exhibiting such beautiful shapes and colors that perhaps they have come from heaven itself. You look with pleasure at the flowers and the vineyard. (Pause.)

Nearby is a white gazebo with an inviting bench covered with bright cotton cushions. You walk to this gazebo and sit comfortably. In the distance, you begin to see a man walking toward you. Why, it is Jesus! Your friend. You are so happy; you rise and go to meet him. Take some time now and see Jesus as he appears in the vineyard. See his hair, his clothes, his tender eyes of love. Looking into these gentle eyes, you take his hand, and together you return to the gazebo to sit upon the bench. Together, you enjoy all the sights and sounds of the vineyard and the gardens. Birds are singing, and nearby, a little brook whispers as it falls over the rocks. (Pause.)

Gently, Jesus says to you, "Remember, I am the vine and you, my dear one, are the branch. I want you to stay with me, close to me, and let me love you. I give you my life. It will be new life springing up within you." (Short pause.)

Filled with his love and his courage, you tell Jesus now all that is within your heart. Look into his warm, kind eyes, and tell him about your hurt and pain, all your problems, and loss. (Long pause.)

There is no criticism in the face of Jesus. He says your name gently. He explains, "Remember, I love you. Cast your burdens upon me. You and I are one; there is no separation between us."

Gratefully, you lift your eyes again to the beauty of nature surrounding you. You know you sit with the one who creates and heals. (Pause.)

You know you need never be alone. Jesus hugs you gently and says your name again. Hear it deeply within your heart.

Jesus says, "Remember, I will always meet you here in the vineyard. You can come at any time. I don't want you to be alone."

He walks slowly away, and you remain, deeply at peace, in the vineyard. The very plants seem to speak your name. Your heart is filled with a warm and sweet light. It seems that this light is big enough to fill the whole world. This light is love. (Pause.)

This meditation will end in three minutes.

This meditation is ending now.

Open your eyes and return to this place, knowing that the vineyard will always be there for you. You can return at any time.

(To conclude, you may want to play, "In the Garden," available on *Catholic Classics,* Vol. VII from GIA Publications.)

Week Six

GROUNDED IN SPIRIT: OUR IMAGES OF GOD

Gathering

The altar area features icons, some seasonal items as appropriate, and candles. If anyone has an icon of the Trinity, it would be a wonderful addition for this meeting.

The group gathers and chats for a moment.

The leader is chosen for this meeting and lights the candle, inviting the group to relax and center, possibly by focusing on the candlelight.

Opening Prayer

Leader: Holy Spirit, come into our gathering this day and make Christ known to each of us. Plant new life within our barren places; fill us with Jesus so that we may be your vessels, bearing your presence to all we meet.

Response: Amen.

Leader: Lord, I hear what you are telling me, you are sending me to speak peacefully to every person I meet.

Response: Show us your kindness, Lord.

Leader: Kindness and truth are meeting now, Lord. Justice is coming and peace is near! You are pouring out your benefits and opening your arms in salvation.

Response: Show us your kindness, Lord.

Leader: May we prepare your way, Lord. May we await your coming with peace.

Response: Show us your kindness, Lord.

Leader: Justice and peace shall meet in our hearts and embrace. You are making all things new!

Response: Show us your kindness, Lord.

Observe a moment of silence.

Activity

A large sheet of white paper is provided, and perhaps a poster board or two if needed. Each participant is given a colored marker. On the posters, write your different images or names of God, both those you consider negative and those positive. Everyone writes at once in a disorganized fashion; some names may be upside down or sideways. Be free.

(Examples: lover, judge, mother, creator-king, list

maker and so on.)

After the posters are finished, display them in the altar area. Discuss how different images of God can arise.

Activity

Form into pairs and discuss with your partners your journaling for the week. Choose different partners than you did in previous weeks.

Break

Break for conversation and refreshments.

Discussion

When the group comes together again, go around the circle and ask the members to name their dominant image of God. Then go around and have them each name a shadow image, an image that still lurks in their mind, even though they don't wish it to. The question: How to heal unhealthy, shadow images of God?

Allow time for meditation to music and silent prayer.

Looking Ahead

Discuss the next meeting and preview next week's material. Ask the members to bring in pictures of themselves at various ages for next week.

Closing Prayer

Close with prayers around the circle and a sign of peace.

Week Seven

GROUNDED IN REALITY: WHO AM I, REALLY?

Gathering

As the group gathers, have members place on the altar area the photographs they brought.

Opening Prayer

Leader: Lord, bless our prayer journey with you; open our lips to speak your truth. May we speak gently and kindly, holding in love ourselves and others. Amen.

Discussion

Leader: What is our ego? Our ego is not a bad thing. It is the executive function of our personalities. It tries to keep us safe and to help us succeed. Sometimes, however, the ego is too separate from the God within us. The ego wants its own way, and it ignores what God wants for our lives. Our ego can drive us and make us want success and "looking good" above all other values.

Invite any comments about ego and our inner experience with ego.

Now members turn in their journals as needed and discuss the following questions. (If needed, review the rules for group process.)

Do you believe that you are made in God's image? Why or why not?

What did you discover about the real and the false self?

How did you react to the reading about shame?

How do we know when we are acting authentically?

Activity

Going around the circle, group members turn to the person on their right and announce one admirable quality about that person. For example, "You listen well; I feel comfortable with you." Take turns so that everyone hears an affirmation.

Break

Break for refreshments and conversation.

Gather and preview next week's chapters. For the next meeting, the leader needs to have copies or a recording of "Amazing Grace."

Ritual

Each person takes a picture of someone else from the altar area and holds the picture throughout the ritual.

Leader: We are made in God's image, and we seek to find the light within us.

Response: We are made in God's image, and God sees that we are good.

Leader: Let us live out of our light and rejoice in our gifts.

Response: We are made in God's image, and God sees that we are good.

Leader: We each hold the picture of someone who is made, as we are, in God's image.

Response: We are made in God's image and God sees that we are good.

Leader: Please bless this picture now with the sign of the cross. (Each member blesses the picture she is holding. The leader then returns the picture to its owner, and offers that person a sign of peace.)

Closing Prayer

Join hands and pray the Lord's Prayer.

Week Eight

GROUNDED IN WHOLENESS: JOHN 9

Gathering

Group gathers around the altar area where a Bible is open to John 9. Have a simple bowl containing some water and a small towel at the ready.

Choose readers to be: Jesus, Narrator, the neighbor(s), the Pharisee(s), the parent(s), the blind man.

Opening Prayer

Read John 9 aloud, with the people chosen above reading the appropriate verses. Be sure to use expression. Let your acting sense have play. Enjoy this.

Discussion

Turn to journaling pages for the week.

* Which character in this passage do you identify with most?
* Which one do you most *not* want to resemble. Why?
* Does this make you react when you see this personality in yourself or others? Explain.

Observe silent meditation for five minutes. Play quiet background music if desired. End this discussion period by playing or singing the song "Amazing Grace." If any member plays the guitar, this is an easy song to play.

Break

Break for refreshments and conversation.

Looking Ahead

Gather the group and preview next week's lesson. Ask members to bring symbols of healing to the next meeting.

Ritual

As soft music plays, each person, one at a time, dips his fingers into the bowl of water and gently makes the sign of the cross over another member's closed eyes. Continue until everyone has given and received the water sign. Then offer each other a sign of peace.

Closing Prayer

O God, I know that all is gift and all comes from you.
May this water heal my blindness.
May I see the goodness in myself and others.
Let new life grow in my heart,

nourished by your warm and gentle
healing rain. Amen.

Share good-bye hugs all around!

Week Nine

SURROUNDING OURSELVES WITH HEALING

(Note: A small amount of scented oil is needed for this meeting. You can use baby oil and scent it with perfume, or purchase healing oils from a bookstore or similar shop.)

Gathering

The group gathers around an altar that is decorated with symbols of healing. These could include an icon of Christ, some water in a pitcher, some greenery and perhaps some rocks and sand. Do as much or as little with décor as you like. Often there is a person in the group who enjoys putting décor together and has an innate sense of what is needed.

Light a candle before beginning.

Opening Prayer

Read John 4.

Leader: Lord, you met the woman at the well, who asked you how you could know everything about her heart. We ask you today, Lord. Can you heal our hearts?

Response: Give us living water, Lord, so that we may not thirst again.

Leader: She was an outcast, Jesus, but you saw her heart. Help us to welcome the outcast within our midst. The parts of us we push away, the people we don't want to claim.

Response: Give us living water, Lord, so that we may not thirst again.

Leader: For you know everything about us, Lord, and

you offer to wash us clean, fill us with new life, and never leave us thirsting. Be near to us now, Jesus, draw near and touch our hearts.

Response: Give us living water, Lord, so that we may not thirst again.

Discussion

The leader asks the group to turn to this week's pages in their journals and the book. The leader asks these questions:

- How did you respond to these healing stories of Jesus? Which one resonated most with you and why?
- Is there any specific healing in your life that you would like the group to pray for?
- Is low self-esteem a problem for you?
- In what ways is God touching you during your daily prayer?

Ask for a volunteer to read one of the closing prayers from the week's pages, or a prayer they have written.

Break

Break for conversation and coffee.

Looking Ahead

Discuss pages in book to be read next, and plans for next meeting.

Ritual

Reassemble the group. Center with a moment of silence. Play or sing a song such as "Peace Is Flowing Like a River" or "Heal Me, Yahweh" by Vince Ambrossetti.

The leader begins by tracing a cross with the healing oil on the forehead of the person behind him or her, saying, "May you be healed by the love of our God." This person takes the oils and crosses the forehead of the next person, saying, "May you be healed by the love of our God." (Continue until each member has received the cross of oil.)

Closing Prayer

Lord, you are wonderful,
And all your works are wonderful.
We thank you for your healing touch within our hearts.
We thank you for the presence of each one here.
Our love grows for each other,
And for you.
Keep us safe and enfolded in your grace
Until we meet once more.
Amen.

Week Ten

SURROUNDING OURSELVES WITH FORGIVENESS

Gathering

The group gathers around the altar area. On a simple card, the leader has written the word "Forgiveness." This card is placed on the altar. The leader asks everyone to sit and to begin to breathe in silence, tuning in to the breath. The leader suggests that on the inhale the group think the word "Abba," and on the exhale, the word "Trust." The group continues in this way for five or more minutes.

Opening Prayer

Leader: Lord, I cannot even try to comprehend how you forgave those who hurt you so, even putting you on a cross to die a painful death. It is a mystery I hold in my heart. It makes me ashamed of how little it takes in my life to build walls of resentment and unforgiveness. And yet, I know you understand. You always understand. If there is a way tonight, let me take my walls down, just a little.

Response: Show me the way, my Lord. Show me the way. Amen.

Discussion

Is there anyone who will share the struggle to forgive as it has unfolded for you? (Details of conflicts may be kept vague as each member shares.)

Continue the discussion. Members may want to say what stage of forgiveness they are in, or explain how they were able to forgive someone.

(Note: If the members want to keep details vague, this does not impact the process at all. This is about the inner process.) At end of discussion, hold hands and recite the Lord's Prayer.

Looking Ahead

Discuss the next meeting and logistics. Turn to needed pages in the book and look over them. Ask members to bring crosses from their homes to the next meeting. Since many people have decorative crosses in their homes, this should not be a difficult task. Just bring what is easy to bring.

Break

Have a break for coffee and conversation.

Ritual

Items needed for ritual: a paper bag or similar container labeled "God's Bag," 3 x 5 index cards, markers and an instrumental CD.

Give each member an index card and a marker. As soft music plays, the member writes on the card the name of someone who she or he is struggling to forgive. If desired, the member can write, "a friend," or "a teacher," instead of a name. As soft music continues to play, the members sit for some moments, praying over what they have written. The card is then folded and placed in "God's Bag." Do all this slowly, reverently.

Leader: God, you see the names, and you know the stories. Now we place all these issues in your bag. Hold them and heal us. We continue to pray about them, and about the state of our hearts. But we know that all this is not up to us. You will gift us with graces that help us to forgive. Thank you, God. Thank you.

Closing Prayer

End with holding hands and offering spontaneous prayer. Share hugs all around or some other sign of peace.

(Note: One very trusted member of the group may offer to take the bag home and burn it. Or the group may want to discuss where the bag should remain. Another possibility is to bring the bag to the next meeting and burn it there. Variations on any ritual are fine; you may have a different or better way to do this.)

Week Eleven

IMMERSED IN THE PASCHAL MYSTERY

Gathering

The group members gather around an altar that is bare except for candles. The group practices centering prayer in silence for a few minutes.

Opening Prayer

The meeting opens with the Lord's Prayer.

Activity

Choose a partner at random, perhaps one you have not worked with. The partners discuss the week's experiences with one another. Spend at least thirty minutes doing this, or more as needed. Individuals should take the opportunity to read from their journals to their partner if desired. Remember not to try to fix one another. Listen to each other with intensity and caring.

Break

Break for coffee and conversation.

Looking Ahead

The leader asks for comments from the group about this week's insights or experiences. Discuss the material for the upcoming week. The members pick up the crosses they brought from home and prepare for the following ritual.

Ritual

Leader: We bring our crosses tonight
To place upon your altar.
You know them well, God.
They hold people, and events and facts in our lives
That we cannot control and make fit as we would like.
Unforgiveness and brokenness,
Ugliness and pain.
Depression and addiction, anger and grief.
And yet, in our cross is resurrection.
You are dying, yet rising in our lives, Dear Jesus.
In all our lives. Amen.

As soft music plays, group members one by one place their cross or crosses on the table. If anyone has forgotten to bring a cross or doesn't have one, share! As each cross is placed on the altar, the group members remain around the table, praying silently. Some groups may want to embrace each member as that member places the cross on the table.

Closing Prayer

Hold hands in silence. Offer prayers of petition or any prayer from the heart as individuals, in no particular order.

Week Twelve

WELCOMING THE CALL OR RESISTING?

Gathering

Group members gather around the altar with books and prayer journals.

If appropriate, the altar area may be decorated for Advent or with icons of Mary and Jesus. Candles and green plants may be used.

The members turn to the prayer ritual for this meeting in their books.

The leader lights the candle and invites the group to center themselves and release the pressures of the day, being fully present in the circle.

Opening Prayer

Leader: My soul magnifies my Lord.

Response: And my spirit rejoices in God my Savior.

Leader: For he has looked upon his lowly one.

Response: And my spirit rejoices in God my Savior.

Leader: The almighty has done great things for me, and holy is God's name!

Response: And my spirit rejoices in God my Savior.

Leader: He lifts up the lowly; his mercy is forever and forever!

Response: And my spirit rejoices in God my Savior.

If appropriate, play some instrumental music for Advent. The Notre Dame Folk Choir has two beautiful Advent recordings. Or use "O Come, O Come Emmanuel," or a similar song. Allow the group to meditate for five minutes as the music plays.

Discussion

The leader invites members to turn in their prayer journals to Week Three, Day Seven. The sharing does not proceed in any particular order. The leader may read the questions from day seven of prayer aloud if needed. If there is no comment on a particular question, don't hesitate to move on. Remember that not all questions need be covered.

The leader brings the discussion to a close as needed before the meeting needs to end. It is important that meetings start and end on time.

As the discussion ends, the leader invites the group to sit in silence for five minutes. Music may be played.

Break

Break for coffee if desired.

Looking Ahead

Come back to the circle and discuss the logistics for the next meeting. If desired, offer petitions to God around the circle.

Closing Prayer

All: Dear God, we love you. You are as close as our breath, as wide as the sky. You hold us close and you comfort us. We all pray for our brothers and sisters present here and the families represented here. Keep us secure in our changes. Keep us near you as we journey on together. Amen.

Week Thirteen

THE CALL: LEARNING TO LOVE AS GOD LOVES

(Note: The group has now established intimacy and core values. Those who were not ready for this journey have fallen away. Not a lot of structure will be needed at this time. Comments will come freely and easily in a spirit of acceptance and community.)

Opening Prayer

You may wish to open the meeting with a praise song, such as "Glory and Praise to Our God," "The Spirit Is a' Moving," or "We are Called."

Discussion

If the group is large, you may wish to break into small groups of three or so to discuss the following questions:

• Does the writing about call make sense to you in your life?
• What, specifically does it mean to you?
• Are you able to live each day with some measure of Joy? Why or why not?
• Is healing becoming apparent in your life? In what ways?
• Are you handing things differently now? Are relationships improving?

Break

Break for coffee and conversation.

Looking Ahead

The leader gathers the group and asks for closing comments. Discuss the next meeting, which is the next-to-last session. Group members will plan the next meeting to fit their needs. Arrange how this will be done.

Ritual

Play soft music and sit in silence for a few minutes.

Then go around the circle, with each person reading one of the following:
- Dear Lord, Thank you for your gift of healing.
- Abba, Daddy, thank you for your gifts and call in my life.
- Holy Spirit, thank you for joy and life and all good things.
- We pray for our families (pause).
- We pray for our friends (pause).
- We pray for our broken and bleeding world (pause).
- Let us be Christ in the world.
- Let us bring love to the world.
- Let us go forth without fear.
- Let us be light in the world.

Closing Prayer

Holding hands, recite the Lord's Prayer.
Share hugs or signs of peace all around.

Week Fourteen

LIVING WITH GOD PRESENT NOW

This meeting will be planned and executed by the group members. Be sure everyone is involved. It may be a time that many will read from their journals. It may be a thanksgiving event.

You may want to have a deacon come for a communion service, or a priest, if available, may offer the sacraments of reconciliation, healing and/or Eucharist. A speaker, someone who is living the call, may be invited also. Plan what the group wants and needs. Any of the prayers from the book can be incorporated here.

Week Fifteen

LIVING AND LOVING WITH FREEDOM . . . REJOICE!

It is suggested that the group celebrate the ending of a journey at this meeting. You may want to meet at a restaurant or a member's home to break bread together. Party games or music may be the order of the day. Or if this doesn't feel right, meet for Mass together and then go out to breakfast or lunch. You decide what your group prefers. Choose joy. Choose life. Love one another.

The Journey Ends?

Your group has now come to the end of its prayer journey. It will not be unusual for groups to continue to meet. Deep bonds have been formed and members may want to see one another on a regular basis. Some groups may want to discuss the lectionary readings of the week and the ways their lives are touched by the principles found in the readings. Other groups may choose books with journaling and reflection questions so that they may continue the inner prayer journey that this book has brought them to.

Sometimes groups will fade away. All of this is natural and there is no perfect way to sustain a group or let it go. Your instincts will guide you as will your prayer. You may feel called to start a new group with other people you know or members of your church.

You can continue with one member of the group as a prayer partner, meeting on a regular basis to discuss your life of prayer. This kind of support is vital to this pilgrim life of inner work.

I will continue to pray for all of you and hold you close in my heart.

Go in peace.
Go in perfect freedom.
You are safe.
You are loved.
All is well.
—*Lyn*

Notes

1. Harold S. Kushner, *The Lord Is My Shepherd: Healing Wisdom of the Twenty-Third Psalm* (New York: Knopf, 2003), p. 60.

2. Paula D'Arcy, *Seeking with All My Heart: Encountering God's Presence Today* (New York: Crossroad, 2003), p. 120.

3. Paula D'Arcy, *Gift of the Red Bird: The Story of a Divine Encounter* (New York: Crossroad, 2002), p. 94–95.

4. Thomas Keating, *Awakenings* (New York: Crossroad, 1990), p. 52.

5. Julia Cameron, *The Artist's Way: A Spiritual Path to Higher Creativity* (New York: Tarcher, 2002), p. 94.

6. John Bradshaw, *Family Secrets: The Path to Self-Acceptance and Reunion* (New York: Bantam, 1996), p. 30.

7. Phillip Bennett, *Let Yourself Be Loved* (Mahwah, N.J.: Paulist, 1997), p. 55.

8. Henri Nouwen, quoted in *All Shall Be Well* (New York: The Berkley Publishing Group, 2004), p. 22.

9. Joyce Rupp, *May I Have This Dance?* (Notre Dame, Ind.: Ave Maria Press, 1992), p. 83.

10. Richard Rohr, *Everything Belongs: The Gift of Contemplative Prayer* (New York: Crossroad, 2003), pp. 69–70.

11. Cameron, p. 30.

12. Keating, p. 36.